THE SUPERWOMAN'S SURVIVAL GUIDE

Conquering the Unexpected in the Office, on the Town, or in the Great Outdoors

KY FURNEAUX

SKYHORSE PUBLISHING

Skyhorse Publishing books may be purchased in bulk at special discounts for sales promotion, corporate gifts, fund-raising, or educational purposes. Special editions can also be created to specifications. For details, contact the Special Sales Department, Skyhorse Publishing, 307 West 36th Street, 11th Floor, New York, NY 10018 or info@skyhorsepublishing.com.

Skyhorse® and Skyhorse Publishing® are registered trademarks of Skyhorse Publishing, Inc.®, a Delaware corporation.

Visit our website at www.skyhorsepublishing.com.

All photos are from Thinkstock unless otherwise noted.

10 9 8 7 6 5 4 3 2 1

Library of Congress Cataloging-in-Publication Data is available on file.

ISBN: 978-1-62873-662-5

Printed in China

For my Nan, who always told me I should write a book, and for my Gran, who taught me about adventure by leading the way.

CONTENTS

INTRODUCTION

Allow me to introduce myself and explain why I think I may be able to help you survive in this crazy world of ours should disaster strike. My name is Ky Furneaux, and I have worked as an outdoor survival expert and Hollywood stuntwoman for more than twenty years.

I learned very early on that all actions have an equal and opposite reaction. The outdoors can be a very unforgiving place. And mistakes often lead to sudden and obvious results. I found that spending time in nature is a fabulous way of learning life lessons. I also saw that you can't pretend to be someone you aren't in the outdoors (well, not for long, anyway).

My life changed course drastically when I was nineteen. I was studying to become a business management student destined for a life of sitting behind a desk when a car accident altered the course of my life. I remember hearing the crack in my spine as the car hit a concrete pole. As panic erupted all around me, I kept myself focused on the fact that I could still wiggle my toes and feel my arms and legs. This is what kept me going as I was loaded onto a spinal board and taken to the hospital.

At the hospital, X-rays confirmed that I had indeed broken my back. Fortunately, my doctor thought that I would be immobile for only three to six months, and that after an extended period of rehabilitation, I would be all right, although I would have a limited physical capacity for the rest of my life. When I asked what this meant, the doctor muttered something about "no tennis" and went on his way.

When a buddy of mine suggested I try rock climbing to complement my rehab program, I jumped at the opportunity to get back outside and challenge the notion that I would never be fully capable again. Rock climbing is the only sport other than swimming that uses every muscle in the human body, so although it might have seemed like a stupid and risky choice, it was probably one of the best ways to heal my damaged body.

While I finished my degree in business management, I also trained myself to be a rock-climbing instructor and entered the world of being an outdoor guide. Over the next ten years, I spent more than three hundred nights a year in the outdoors. I became a kayaking, sailing, hiking, and rappelling guide. I worked with corporate groups, schoolkids, juvenile offenders, and the general public, teaching them skills and giving them the opportunity to change their lives by facing their fears and overcoming their limitations in the outdoors.

I also faced my own fears and limitations out there on a regular basis. The outdoors can be scary. It's extremely unpredictable. There are things that can kill you or physically harm you. I had the mindset that I never wanted to be scared of anything, so if something scared me, I confronted it until I wasn't scared anymore. I found that most of my fears were based on false beliefs or ignorance. Once I realized this, I worked to alleviate those fears in others.

After working as an outdoor guide, I decided that it would be nice to actually come home to a warm, comfortable bed once in a while. Someone suggested that I become a stunt performer, and it seemed like a natural progression. But the leap from outdoor guide to stuntwoman was a bigger one than I thought.

I had heard that Vancouver, Canada, was being touted as "Hollywood North," so I headed there to begin my new career (I wasn't quite ready for Los Angeles). Someone suggested that I take fight training, and I found myself a mentor for that. Someone else suggested I was way too old (I was twenty-eight), and I ignored that. It took about a year of spending every day doing something that would help me become a stunt performer before I secured my first stunt job. I called my mother and cried. My "impossible dream" was becoming a reality.

Although I have trained in many different areas for my stunt career, the ability to face down my fears is one of the most useful skills I have. A good stunt performer is not necessarily the one who has the fanciest backflip, but the person who can tame her fight-or-flight response.

A stunt performer puts herself into some crazy situations, such as falling out of a building backward or allowing flames to consume her clothing. I listened to the voice in my head that said, "Run away!" and ignored it as I threw myself down a flight of stairs. I had to be able to get up and do it all over again if the director felt like the camera angle just wasn't right. After doing this for a while, I realized how far the human body can be pushed and still go on. Too often in the past, I had given up on something that I could have achieved by pushing a little harder. I eventually even overcame my fear of Los Angeles and made the move to Hollywood.

While working as a stunt performer, I continued to spend time in the outdoors. It was where my soul came most alive. I continued to educate myself about

different countries and climates. What were the local indigenous foods and medicines in North America compared to those of my native Australia? Did the land still provide sustenance in places where human habitation had swelled to epic proportions? How could I survive and thrive in harsh, cold conditions unlike any that I had experienced in my homeland?

I believe that if we are faced with a true survival situation, chances are we will end up facing nature and depending on it to survive. I also believe that even in the smallest emergency, say a three-hour power outage or a storm that shuts the city down for a day, if you are confident, you will make good decisions that will ensure your own safety as well as those around you. I'm a firm believer that the person who will survive the longest will not be the person who has bought enough bottled water to last a week or two, but rather the person who can treat and gather her own water.

I have spent a lot of time in situations where my life and the lives of those around me have depended on the decisions I make and my mental state. I have learned the hard way what works and what doesn't. I'd like to share my experiences with you so that you and your loved ones don't have to step into the flames to find out what burns.

In my experience coming out on top in an unexpected situation is mostly about attitude and adaptation. I believe in being educated and prepared so you can be confident in yourself and your abilities. You will be fine if nothing happens, and let me tell you, I am all for believing in a shiny, happy future. But with preparation you will also be fine if something *does* happen. It's better and more empowering to act rather than react whether you are unexpectedly heading a large international sales meeting or facing down a bear at your campfire.

So, with that in mind, I've structured my book around four guiding principles that will help you survive in any situation, from the office, to the urban jungle, to the great outdoors.

My Four Principles of Survival

- Think Positive – It's all a matter of your 'tude, so be the best you can be
- Be Prepared – Develop skills and strategies to cope with the unexpected
- Be Adaptable – Know how to assess, plan, and respond
- Educate Yourself – Knowledge is power, so use your head

There are plenty of manuals out there that will teach you how to tie knots and how many ramen noodle packets to put in your cellar. This book is not one of those. It is a guide rather than a manual. Sure, I've included what I consider to be the most helpful survival hints, but what I really want to do is inspire you to develop the attitude and flexibility necessary to survive a variety of situations. And who knows, these life principles may help you move more smoothly through your everyday life.

Chapter 1
THINK POSITIVE

Your best weapon

The best self-defense is not a good offense; rather, it's never to get yourself into a bad situation in the first place. If you are confident with your own knowledge and abilities, you will make good decisions and ensure your own safety and that of those around you.

In all survival situations, you will need to assess your ability to get access to water, food, fire, and shelter and then plan accordingly. These are your basic needs and without them you will not survive.

In the city, you will need to be able to read situations correctly and respond with the right tactics, attitude, and skills.

*The best weapon that you always carry with you is your mind!

Studies have shown that the people who have the best attitude toward whatever situation they find themselves in generally fare better than those with the best survival gear. I also find that anyone who prefers to make the most of whatever happens is usually a good friend to have around!

Your limits

People often stop before they have actually reached their limits of trying. This is more commonly known as "giving up." I felt so passionate about the fact that the land could still provide all that we needed to survive that I helped organize and participated in a documentary-style expedition called "Hike for Survival." A fellow survivalist and I hiked over a hundred miles across the Sierra Nevadas and lived off the land as we did so. The only tool we took was a multi-tool pocketknife. We slept on the ground, made fire from friction, ate and drank only what we found out there, and hiked vast distances in the ten days it took to traverse the Sierras from the west to the east.

This was when I truly realized that we have all we need to survive in nature and that the things we surround ourselves with in the modern world, although of great comfort, are not necessary for survival. I walked out the other side of the mountain range fitter, healthier, and happier than I had been in a long time. Sure, I looked like I needed a good meal and rushed to the nearest Starbucks for my vanilla soy latte, but I had thrived out there, both mentally and physically.

My point? Our bodies adapt. They can take much more punishment and can give out much more energy than we give them credit for. It is our minds that interfere, suggesting (often simply out of habit) that we are tired and hungry, and that we can't do this because we never have before.

Know your limits but also know that what you perceive as your limits is probably only just the beginning of your strength and resilience.

In a situation where your survival depends on your ability to gather one more armload of firewood, or hike across one more valley before dark, chances are you have it in you to keep going despite the fact that you feel absolutely exhausted.

A good time to begin to practice knowing what you are capable of is when you are not in a survival situation. Try staying in a yoga pose for ten seconds longer than usual. On a run, take a break at the top of the hill instead of in the middle. Walk to the grocery store instead of getting in your car. Chances are, you will manage it and the rush you get from achieving more than you thought you could will be its own reward.

I have pushed my body and mind in some situations far beyond what I had previously thought they could do. I have not yet found a situation in which I have fallen down and absolutely could not go on. I may have needed to rest and regroup for a moment, but I have always been able to get up again. I believe that we all have that ability within us.

The comfort zone (and getting out of it)

The comfort zone is a behavioral state within which a person operates in an anxiety-neutral condition. It's usually a situation without a sense of risk. People who always operate within their comfort zones rarely achieve the high levels of success that someone who takes risks does. They don't end up having the dramatic "failures" that those risks can sometimes result in either. I personally prefer to be on the side of trying and "failing" rather than never having tried at all.

As people age, their comfort zones usually become smaller and smaller. This results in living a life that is bound by routine. But the opposite can happen as well. You can consciously and deliberately expand the walls of your comfort zone and find that things that previously would have made you anxious now don't affect you adversely at all (and you may even come to enjoy them).

The way that I expand my comfort zone is by doing the things I fear. I was once scared

The thing with comfort zones is that they are actually quite fluid.

of spiders, but because I encountered quite a number of big, hairy ones in the outdoors, I made myself watch them and hold them and find beauty in them (yes, beauty). I now can pick up most spiders to carry them out of my house or tent.

I used to be very nervous about speaking in front of large numbers of people. I got over this by making sure that I knew the topic I was speaking

about inside out and then forced myself to con-front my fear head-on. I was terrified at first, but now I think nothing of it.

If something unexpected has happened to you "out of the blue," you're probably experiencing something outside your comfort zone. Take cour-age when in this state and trust that you'll make the right decisions. Once you start expanding your comfort zone, you may be tempted to keep going!

Attitude

Except for very extreme circumstances, I believe that no one can make you unhappy. And I believe that choosing to be unhappy ultimately only ends up ruining your own experience.

We all choose the attitude we adopt in life. Why not choose a positive attitude rather than a destructive or negative one? Adopt an attitude that empowers you, and you will gain power from it, in both your normal life and in survival situations.

Choosing to be negative about a situation puts the focus on the bad things about the experience. If you are in a survival situation, chances are that you may be cold, tired, and hungry, but focus-ing on those things will not make them go away. Choose instead to focus on the things you do have, such as being alive and coherent. Looking at the

things that are working for you will help you figure out how best to deal with the situation. It will allow you to discover your strengths and then use them to your advantage.

There is a difference between focusing on the negative and assessing your weaknesses. An example of focusing on the negative is complaining that you are cold. An example of assessing your weaknesses is realizing that you are sitting near the top of a cold mountain. By being on a cold mountain, you are exposing your body to elements such as wind and rain. Noting that this is a weakness in your survival plan will allow you to make a strategy and act, by moving to a warmer position out of the wind, for instance.

"Good pain" versus "bad pain"

Bad pain is something that makes an injury worse, and whatever activity is causing that pain should be stopped immediately. Good pain (which is actually most pain) can bring about positive change. Examples of good pain include a deep tissue massage, the breakdown of scar tissue, and the exercise of a muscle that has not been used for a while. Many people feel pain and just stop doing whatever it is that is causing them that pain. This can be worse for

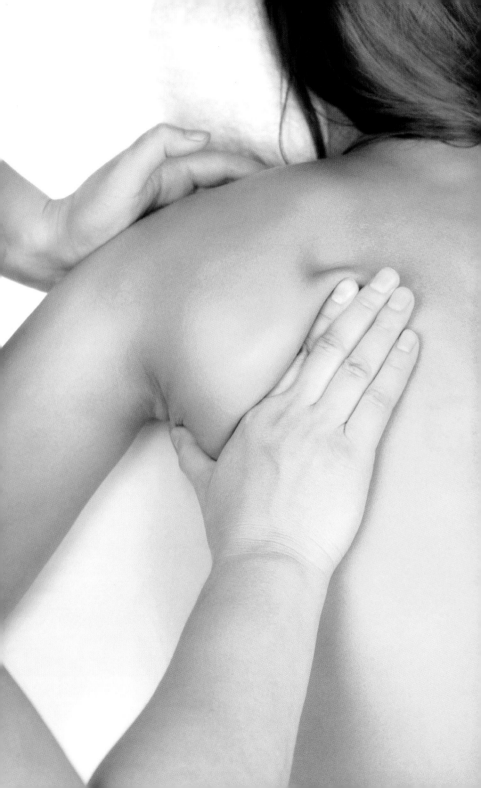

the muscle in the long run and can cause atrophy and permanent damage.

As a stuntwoman, I have often thought that there should be as many words for "pain" as the Inuit supposedly have for "snow." Out of the twenty or so different kinds of pain that I experience on a regular basis, there are really only one or two that stop me in my tracks and require immediate and urgent attention, like the time I tore a ligament in my foot while working on *Thor*. Within five minutes, it was so swollen and sore that I couldn't put any weight on it at all. Doctors told me I would be on crutches for six weeks, but I had a stunt to perform the following day, so I dosed up on painkillers, wrapped my foot tightly, and hobbled out there to do my job anyway.

Most of the time I experience just the good pain of my body pushing itself as it heals from injury or builds up the muscles necessary for me to complete a stunt sequence—or fit into a skintight

The next time you feel pain, assess it a little before you stop what you are doing. It may just be doing you some good.

superhero suit! If I stopped every time I felt pain, I would never get out of bed! I have just gotten very good at knowing which pain is doing me good and which pain is injuring me further.

Small steps

When faced with a huge personal goal, it can sometimes feel like your own Everest. Do what any climber does when faced with a mountain—take it one small step at a time.

I use this idea whenever I start a new project. I have pretty big dreams, and sometimes, if I look at the whole picture I get too scared to even begin. When I wanted to become a stuntwoman I didn't know how to go about it. I didn't know any stunt performers, and there certainly wasn't a manual out there with any advice. I asked around until I found someone who knew a stunt performer and then finally managed to track him down. I then asked him to tell me everything he knew about how I could make it in this elusive trade. He gave me so much advice that I almost ran away, but then I took a deep breath and made a list: Headshot. I could find someone to take that. Training. I could find someone to help with that. A demo reel. I could borrow a camera and shoot that. All of these goals were manageable chunks and way less intimidating than the big picture. One small step at a time helped me conquer my Everest.

Community

Women are usually the community builders in a social group. They are the ones who remember birthdays, notice when little Billy isn't playing with the others, and kiss the boo-boos to magically make them better.

In a survival situation, a sense of community will help build your morale, and morale will give you a reason to live. It may not be vital in the first twenty-four hours, but as hours stretch to days and possibly into weeks, it will become almost as important as building a good shelter. It may be the difference between giving up and wandering into the desert alone to die or kicking it Swiss Family Robinson-style until the ship is spotted on the horizon.

Have a mantra

Say to yourself, "This too shall pass." It's a calming sentence, isn't it? I use this saying in all sorts of situations, from getting through a hard workout at the gym to being so cold I think my toes will need to be amputated at the end of an expedition. The thing to remember about discomfort is that, in most cases, it is only temporary (well, that's the hope, anyway). If you are cold, you will one day be warm again. If it hurts, that pain will stop eventually. If you are thirsty, do the right things and you should be able to find some water before you suffer dehydration.

I use this phrase when I've been to the dentist and had teeth removed. I use it when I want to have an early morning dip in the freezing ocean or when I have forgotten my sweater and don't want to ruin dinner by complaining. Try it. It may help you too.

Presentation

One thing people tend to forget in an emergency situation is presentation. It seems like just a little thing, but I believe it helps greatly with your attitude.

Think about it. There's a reason why you shave your legs, wash your hair, and put on some makeup

and your cutest outfit when you get excited about a fun night out. It makes you feel good!

A survival situation is no different. I'm not telling you to think about presentation before getting the essentials sorted out, but if you do get the chance to bathe or clean your clothes, you will feel much better. This will assist with good sanitary habits, improve your morale, make you feel more alive, and others around you will appreciate it too!

In good shape

It's important to try to break a sweat at least three times a week and get your blood flowing through the body. The bonus is that your clothes will fit

*Look after yourself in the short-term so that you can defend yourself in the long-term. The healthier you are and the better shape your body is in, the more likely you will be able to deal with unexpected situations.

better too. When the number of calories that you burn is greater than the number of calories that you consume, you *will* lose weight.

Every modern girl knows that exercise burns calories. As Jenny Craig will swiftly let you know, most processed food is very high in calories. In a survival situation, after those stockpiled protein bars have run out, you will be living on food that provides quite a low-calorie intake. You may even be rationing whatever you have left. This is great for the figure (you never see any fat on long-term survivors), but it means that you also have to ration your physical exertion because you won't have as much energy as usual.

Predator and prey

What do predators look for in their victims? The answer is that they look for an *attitude of prey*.

Imagine a little bunny grazing in a meadow. It nervously sniffs around, jumping at every little noise. It looks like it couldn't hurt a fly. In fact, it looks like a fly could perhaps do it some damage. Now imagine a cat walking through that same meadow. It walks with grace and assurance that it knows how to defend itself if need be. Sure, it has sharp teeth and sharp claws, but the eagle above doesn't know that. All it sees are two animals in a

meadow. One looking like it would be easy dinner and one looking like it shouldn't be messed with. I'm guessing the eagle is going to go for the bunny. Human predators operate the same way.

Ironically, the majority of human predators are cowards and bullies. They're usually sneaky in their attack behavior because they like to provoke fear in others. So if you can muster it, a show of aggression can deter attack. Don't act like a victim and you may well end up not being the victim. When I traveled through Africa, I was told

Human predators are generally cowards who prey on those they perceive to be weak and vulnerable. If you have an air of confidence about you, you are more likely to be left alone.

that if I found myself about to be attacked by a lion, I was not to show fear. I was to make myself seem bigger, wave my arms around aggressively, and yell loudly. This would apparently confuse the lion and deter attack. Thank goodness I've never had to test this theory, because I'm pretty sure my flight mechanism would kick in and I'd end up some big kitty's dinner.

Women and pain

Researchers have found that estrogen can act as a natural painkiller. The higher your estrogen level, the higher your pain tolerance. The thing to remember is that pain-numbing endorphins take a second to kick in. The body needs to register the pain with the brain, which then sends a signal to the pituitary gland and hypothalamus to release those endorphins. So after you have slammed your finger in the door, take a second, breathe, and know that the pain will soon pass or at least be bearable much faster than it would for someone with less estrogen (i.e., men).

Among a lot of other scientific research, the Discovery Channel's popular television show *Myth-Busters* actually proved that women have a greater tolerance for pain than men. They did this by seeing who could hold his or her hand in a bowl of ice water for the longest.

I had heard of all kinds of people pushing through painful situations that would normally floor

The mind is amazing at "shelving" the pain until you are in a place to deal with it.

the average person and not noticing how injured they were until later. I didn't think I had that kind of tolerance for pain, but after spending years in the outdoors and doing stunt after stunt, I realized we all have that potential. My body has been bruised and battered, but I don't realize the extent of my injuries until I am soaking in the bathtub.

So, remember, women are naturally bursting with powerful endorphins just waiting to kick in and help us get through painful physical situations. This is a definite bonus in survival situations, as they often require putting physical discomfort and pain aside in order to do what's needed to make it out alive.

"I can't" (which is also known as "I won't try")

I can't flap my arms and fly. That is the truth and until some technology develops wings I can attach on my back, I am not going to jump off a cliff to test that truth out. I won't try Brussels sprouts. I say I can't eat them, but really it's just the idea of them. And truthfully, I've never even tried them.

My mother was not really a fan of getting into a bathing suit to swim in the ocean. She wasn't really keen on the idea of a wet suit either. She could swim but just wouldn't. When she was sixty-two years old, I took her snorkeling in the Great Barrier Reef. I coaxed her into a wet suit despite her cries of "I can't." And you know what? She found her passion. She loved it more than she had loved anything else she had ever done. She had just missed out on years of it because she wouldn't try it.

I do understand there are things that you probably won't like doing after you've tried them. I really don't like the taste of raw tadpoles, and I probably won't be eating them again unless I am dying.

How many things in your life do you say that you can't do? That you feel are not possible, but that you really haven't even tried? What are you missing out on because you are unwilling to give it a go, test it out, and see if you would perhaps like it?

As Jim Carrey found out in *Yes Man*, it can be incredibly freeing to try different things. Who knows? You might find your passion where you least expect it.

What's done is done

In a survival scenario, time spent on regrets is time not spent making the current situation better or livable. I always try to look at what happened objectively and say to myself, "Okay. That happened. Now what?" Yelling, screaming, or throwing things wastes valuable energy, just like sulking, crying, or complaining wastes valuable time.

When I was on the "Hike for Survival," my partner and I experienced a GPS malfunction that took us off the edge of the maps we had. We were exhausted, it was day nine of living off the land, and we had about half a liter of water between the two of us. It was close to dark when we found out where we were. We were on the edge of a deep canyon, and our exit was on the other side. We had thought we were almost out, but it turned out we had about five more hours of hiking to go, most of it in the dark. I remember that moment when we identified how much more we had to do. It took all my strength not to cry. It wouldn't have changed anything. My next response was to just stay sitting

Mistakes happen, plans go awry, and we all do things we wish we hadn't. It's how we get back up and keep moving afterward that defines our future moments.

down. I didn't want to walk anymore. I was angry at my partner, as the GPS was his responsibility on this trip, but I knew that yelling at him wouldn't change the outcome either. Instead, I stood up and put one foot in front of the other. As a result, we were able to maintain a harmonious relationship and get out of the canyon.

Now, I'm not telling you to suppress your emotions. That's not a healthy way of doing things either. I'm just saying that you shouldn't dwell on them. Acknowledge that something happened, that it wasn't ideal, that you feel angry, upset, or disappointed about it, and then figure out a proactive way to move forward. Life gets better faster this way.

"You miss 100 percent of the shots you don't take"

You may recognize this quote from hockey great Wayne Gretzky. Even though he's clearly talking about hockey, the metaphor for life in general is hard to ignore. The bottom line is, if you don't try, you have no chance at all of succeeding.

I have always found that being honest with myself and others about an unfamiliar situation leads to less anxiety. For example, you might find yourself being offered an exciting but scary work opportunity. You could explain to the person offering you the chance that you would love to take it because it will be an incredible experience, but also express that you haven't done something like this before and may need guidance, help, or extra time. Don't be afraid to ask for help. Go online, search for ways to achieve your goal, ask your friends and

family to assist you, or do whatever you need to ensure the best possible outcome.

I once auditioned for a commercial that involved a mini-trampoline stunt. Now, I am not a gymnast, but I have done some trampoline work and am pretty good in the air. The stunt was a little complex, and I knew it would be a challenge for me. In order to get myself ready for it, I found a gym, rented a mini trampoline, and practiced every night until I could hit any mark I wanted. I asked my gymnast friends to watch me and help with my form. The stunt went off perfectly and launched my Los Angeles stunt career. That never would have happened if I had not taken a shot at all.

Power poses

Recent studies have confirmed that how we stand not only presents an image to the outside world but also can change how we feel.

Picture a moment of abject sadness. What do you see? Probably someone curling herself into the fetal position. Now picture what a lack of self-confidence looks like. Perhaps someone with her shoulders slumped, her head down, and a lack of eye contact?

Now imagine someone who radiates confidence. How is she standing? Shoulders back? Chin

held high? Certainty in her gaze? Try standing like this. Do you immediately feel a sense that you could take on the world?

Truth is, it doesn't really matter how you feel on the inside. When you stand up tall with your chin held high, people will view you differently, and you, in turn, will begin to feel differently.

Chapter 2
BE PREPARED

Survival tips for the urban jungle

Always carry your purse or bag with the zipper closed and facing your body. This will make it hard for anyone trying to pickpocket you in a crowded space, such as on public transportation or at a busy mall. If you don't have a zipper on your purse or bag, carry it with the flap closed and hold it close to your body. Anything that requires a bit of effort to open will alert you to the fact when someone is trying to relieve you of your treasured possessions and give you time to react and save them.

To avoid costly trips to the chiropractor, change whichever side you normally carry your heavy purse or bag regularly. This will balance out your body and prevent your muscles from over-developing on one side.

To prevent holes in your stockings from becoming unsightly ladders, keep a small bottle of clear nail polish in your purse. As soon as you notice you have a hole in your stocking, dab the edges of the hole with the nail polish and it will stop any further deterioration of your hose.

Always keep a small tube of toothpaste, a toothbrush, and some deodorant handy in your office desk or tote bag. I used to keep one in my stunt bag just in case I had a particularly close-up fight scene after a garlicky lunch. Your coworkers will appreciate it.

Avoid the Marilyn Monroe effect. On a windy day always remember to hold your skirt down with one hand when you hit an intersection in the city (unless you want to show off your new panties!). The wind funnels through the tall buildings, and when it hits the intersections it creates swirling updrafts that may ruffle even the most tailored of skirts.

The most ferocious animals of the urban jungle are the packs of Friday-night businessmen. They are usually seen hanging around bars and taxi stands with their ties loosened and top shirt buttons undone. Up to three are manageable, but once their numbers rise to four or above, avoid them at all costs. They have finished their tightly controlled work week and are ready to let loose and cause havoc.

New to a city? Be sure to stick to well-populated roads and steer clear of smaller streets and alleys. Until you know which streets host those trendy secondhand shops and which alleys host

the local drug deals, it's best not to take a chance with your life.

Traveling by yourself? Wear sunglasses with dark lenses so that it is hard for people to make eye contact with you. If they can't make eye contact with you, they are less likely to approach and hassle you.

Always carry a mix of cash and credit cards. We are living in an age where we have become so dependent on credit cards for all our transactions that there are times when we don't have cash. This could leave you in a very bad bind if you end up in a "cash only" situation, like trying to catch the last bus home.

Don't put all your eggs in one basket. I always try to carry some cash in a separate place than my wallet, even if it's just a five-dollar bill in my back pocket. That way if my purse or wallet gets stolen, I have some money to make a call to cancel my cards or catch the bus home. I also have a twenty in the glove box of my car in case I forget my purse when I've ducked out to get some milk. This saves a trip back home. This also helps when I have used valet parking and forgotten to take some cash out. Just remember to replace it once you have used it.

Not a fan of the sneakers-with-a-business-suit look? Allow a little bit of extra time to get to work or to catch your bus or train. By walking more slowly, you will prevent shin splints or other lower leg strain injuries that are caused and aggravated by power walking in high heels.

Subway safety. If you are traveling when there aren't many people around, don't get on an empty train car. You may love all the privacy and space, but it takes only one misguided human being to get on with you and you could be in trouble. Pick a car that has at least a few people on it already.

Urban Shelter

In some environmental disasters, your house may become your survival shelter. The same rules that apply to your outdoor shelter will apply to your indoor shelter. You need to make sure that it can maintain a survivable temperature. People have been known to die of heat exhaustion in their own homes as temperatures soar and electricity cuts out. Likewise, extreme blizzards that cause power outages for days at a time can also lead to hypothermia and eventually death.

If your house is heating up due to a power outage, cover all your windows, as light coming in equals heat coming in. Remember that heat rises, so head down to the lower levels of a multi-story house or lie on the floor.

Battery-operated fans can help cool down your body temperature. Circulating air makes it easier for the sweat to evaporate from your skin, which is how you eliminate body heat.

If you have advance warning of a power outage, fill all available watertight vessels with water. This includes the bathtub, sinks, and plastic containers. You can soak a towel in water and place it over your body to cool yourself down or wipe a damp facecloth over exposed skin. Areas that lose heat fastest are the head, feet, and wrists. Stored water will also help with your sanitary

needs. If your electricity is out, your toilets won't flush. Don't bother wasting the water for pee, but a bucket of water will help flush down poop if your power outage extends for several days.

In some cases, extreme cold can also lead to power outages. In these cases you want to prevent the heat from leaving your house. Line all your doors and windows with towels and blankets to prevent the heat from escaping. If you have a large house, close off a room that will be your "nest." Pile all the warm things into that one room, and everyone in the house can sleep in there.

It doesn't take much to warm up a small space, so building a cubby or a tent in the middle of the room can be a good idea. Keep your clothes on. It has been shown that trying to warm up someone with hypothermia by getting naked with that person usually results in two cold people. Your best bet to stay warm is to put on more layers, not take them off. As in the case of extreme heat, if you have warning of a power outage, gather as much water as you can. In this case it is for sanitation only.

Surviving through the night

Exposure can kill you faster than dehydration or starvation, and I'm not talking about the type of exposure that celebrities covet. I am talking about exposure to the elements, such as wind, rain, and the chill of the earth that comes with the setting of the sun. You can last up to three days without water, but one night in cold temperatures can kill you.

The night temperature does not even need to drop below freezing to kill. A warm night with a little bit of rain and a breeze can potentially lead to hypothermia. Because of this, I highly recommend that if you can't get a fire going on the first day of your survival situation, make sure that you get a shelter constructed before it gets dark.

There are many different types of survival shelters. If it protects you from the chill of the earth and the elements of the sky, you can call it a survival shelter. I have three favorite types, depending upon the length of time I am out in the wilderness. The longer I am sleeping outdoors, the more time I have to build a better shelter. Let's start with the basics.

THE LEAF BOX

I am sure that this shelter has a more technical name, but this one helps me remember it. If it were late in the day and I suddenly found myself in need of a shelter to get through the night, I would use this one.

It is fairly quick to assemble but has low warmth potential, is not usually that comfortable, and is not very waterproof, so I would not use it in a long-term survival scenario. It will enable you to survive just through a night.

The Leaf Box requires about eight body-length and six body-width pieces of wood. They are laid down in a crosshatch box form, as shown below.

You will then need to fill the box with as many leaves as possible, remembering that when you

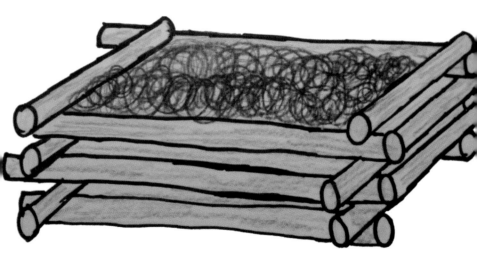

lie on the leaves and branches, they will squish down quite flat. The idea is that you will crawl into the middle of the leaves, so you will need enough to insulate the ground and also to completely cover you to protect you from the elements. If done properly, this has the potential to keep you dry in a rain shower and warm in freezing temperatures.

One thing to be careful of is what types of critters you invite into your Leaf Box for the night. Some piles of leaves may house an ant nest, scorpions, spiders, or other creatures that will make for an uncomfortable night's sleep. But remember, at the end of the day we are looking at survival, not comfort, so the more foliage you can pile into your box, the better.

THE A-FRAME

If I had a day to prepare a shelter for the night, I would choose this one. It is a little more labor intensive than the Leaf Box, but if done properly is more waterproof and windproof.

Its shape is fairly self-explanatory, judging by the name, but there are many ways to build an A-Frame. As I am always aware of burning the least amount of calories possible in a survival scenario, I first look for a situation where the frame has partly constructed itself. Examples of this include a fallen-down tree or a hollowed-out tree trunk. Anywhere one windproof wall is already built will cut down on the labor required. I have learned that rock faces do not usually make good walls in a survival situation, as they generally get very cold at night and suck the warmth away from your body rather than help keep you warm.

The smaller you make this shelter, the better, not only to reduce the time spent making it, but also because your body can warm up a small space faster than a big one.

The final step is to fill the A-Frame with leaves and branches to get your body off the ground and also cover you for warmth. This shelter should be like a little cocoon once you are done.

THE TEEPEE

This shelter is the most labor-intensive shelter, but it is the one I would build should I find myself in a long-term survival scenario in a colder climate.

When built properly it is waterproof, is tall enough to sit in, and gives you the option of having a fire in it that will keep you snug through a very cold night.

There are many ways of building teepees, but the best way I know is to find three long sticks (about six feet long) that each have a fork in the end. Prop the sticks into the ground and intertwine the forks so that the three sticks stand strong and unsupported. Place them wide enough apart so that you can lie down and tall enough so that you can sit underneath them comfortably.

The next step is to find other sticks and fill in the gaps between your three main sticks. Fill in all the gaps you can with sticks and then finish by filling in the remaining gaps with branches and leaves, placing them over the frame you've made. Keep going until you can sit inside and not see any daylight

through the walls. Make sure that you leave a hole to crawl in and out of.

The trick with having a fire in a teepee is to allow a breathing hole in the roof of the teepee for the smoke to escape. If you are in a rainy location, you can waterproof this hole by making a cover from intertwined branches and leaves and placing it over the protruding ends of your frame so it rests about a foot above the hole.

In a space as small as a teepee you will only require a tiny twig fire for warmth during the night. Locate the fire at the center of the teepee and keep it small, or else you may end up burning down your shelter and destroying all your hard work.

The most important thing about any survival shelter is that you cannot see daylight peeping in through it at all when you are lying in it. If you can see daylight peeping in, it is not waterproof.

My final piece of advice applies to any shelter that you build: make sure that you design the entrance to face away from prevailing winds. I always see people build shelters facing the ocean so they can look at the views (I think that's why they do it). But a majority of coastal winds come off the ocean and blow right into their shelters, taking away most of the much-desired warmth. So take a second to think about which way the wind seems to be blowing and place the entrance to your shelter facing the opposite direction. You'll thank me for it in the middle of the night.

Wardrobe malfunction? Fixed!

Replace a broken zipper pull with a paper clip or safety pin so you can zip up that fly in a fix.

When the whole zipper is broken, use a stapler to attach it together again. You will need to use at least one staple for every centimeter that's not working, maybe more if it is a tough material or a tight piece of clothing. The staples will blend in with the zipper and save your dignity.

Have a stuck zipper and urgently need to use the bathroom? Use lip balm or a bar of soap to lubricate the teeth of the zipper for a smoother slide. Coloring the zipper with a pencil will also work if your office supplies are close at hand.

Use double-sided tape to fix up a droopy hem on your skirt. This also works as a temporary replacement for a missing button if your favorite shirt accidentally gets a little too racy on the way to your board meeting. Staples work nicely too but can look a little obvious and unsightly.

Washed your favorite sweater with your fluffy new towels? The unsightly pills can be removed as simply as you would remove the hairs on your legs. Grab a disposable razor and shave the pills off. Quickly and easily, your sweater will look like new.

Broken a heel off your favorite pumps on the way to the office? Superglue works best as a temporary fix, but if there is no glue in sight, some duct tape will hold the heel in place and a permanent marker the color of your shoe will help blend the tape in. It is really important that you don't forget that this is just a temporary fix—walk carefully on your repair job, as it will never be as strong as the real deal. Hit up a shoe repair place at lunchtime

or on the way home. A good repair job can take as little as fifteen minutes.

Water ways

Dehydration can be a killer whether on a simple day hike or an extended trip. It is largely accepted that you can live approximately three days without water, but this can change rapidly depending on other circumstances. If it is hot, you can die without water in less than a single day. If you are exerting a large amount of effort and sweating a lot, you can last even less than that. Even if it is cold and windy, you may be losing more moisture than you think.

My first rule about water is always carry more of it than you think you will need.

Any time I head out for a hike, even if I don't intend to be gone for long, I will take at least a liter. If I am going on a day hike, I will take two, and if it's hot, maybe even three. It may add a bit of weight to your pack, but just think of that as extra weight training and revel in the added calories you will lose—and the extra liquid may just save your life, or someone else's (quite often I end up helping others stave off their heat exhaustion by sharing my water).

But sometimes you may be in a situation where you don't have any water. If you are, you may be near a stream or water source. A general rule of thumb is that any water that is above the ground should be filtered or purified before drinking. In other extremely remote areas around the world, however, I tend to stick to the rule that if it's clear and rapidly flowing, I'll drink it. This hasn't let me down yet.

The best way of making water drinkable is by boiling it. If you have a good fire going and a container to boil the water in, then bringing water to a boil kills any nasty bacteria. Many people have theories as to how long the water needs to boil. The answer is simply that the second the water is at a rolling boil, the bad bacteria die and the water is ready to drink (although you may want to let it cool down first).

If the water is murky or full of sediment, pour it through a T-shirt or similar item of clothing to filter out the gunk before boiling it. Chewing your water down is never fun.

If you are unable to get a fire burning, but have had a fire in the past or happen to be in an area where a bushfire has swept through, you can use the fire's by-product (charcoal) to fashion a home-made water filter. This should not be your first choice, as it may not be 100 percent effective, but it is better than sucking the water straight out of a stream or puddle.

In some kind of open-ended container, place alternate layers of charcoal, grass, and sand. It works best when the container comes to a point or tapers to a smaller end (as shown below). Passing the water through the sand and grass will remove the sediment from the water, and the charcoal should kill any bacteria.

Interestingly, charcoal is also a good remedy for upset stomachs and bloating. Crumble some into a powder and mix with water. It can be eaten to help eliminate toxins if you suspect you have consumed something that may have poisoned your system.

Iodine is commonly found in first aid kits, as it is great for disinfecting cuts. It can also be used to

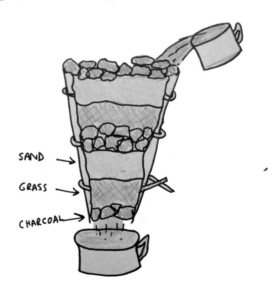

SAND

GRASS

CHARCOAL

clean your water, but it can leave it tasting kind of funny. A good rule of thumb is to add five to ten drops per liter, let sit for five minutes, and then drink.

People with thyroid problems should try to avoid drinking water with iodine in it. However, if it means that you will survive to see another day, you can deal with your thyroid issues when you are back in civilization.

Other water sources

It is not always the case that you will find your-self near an accessible water source. The absolute basics about finding water where it may not be obvious are as follows:

- Vegetation cannot grow without a water source.
- Vegetation cannot grow lush and green without a slightly larger water source.
- Vegetation cannot grow tall without an even larger water source.

What does this mean for you? Look for a rise in the landscape—a small hill or mound will probably do—and walk up it. This will give you a good view of the land around you. If you see an area with tall, lush, green vegetation, it's a good bet that you will find water there.

If the water is not above ground and obvious once you have made your way to the nearest green patch around, there are a few methods that can help you quench your thirst.

DIGGING FOR WATER

If the vegetation patch you have discovered is in or near a dry creek bed, there is a good chance there's water still in that creek bed, but it is just underground. Look for damp mud or soil patches and dig there. Soon your hole should start to fill with muddy water. Allow the sediment to settle before drinking it. You can also strain the water through your clothing if you are desperate.

If there are no moist patches, try digging on the outside of the bends in the dry river. When the river did have surface water, these areas were where it was slowest moving, so water is more likely to have seeped into the underlying ground.

It is not unreasonable that you may need to dig for a foot or so before water appears. If it hasn't appeared by then, try a hole in another location.

LEAF CONDENSATION

If you have a plastic bag of any sort, then this method is a good way to collect drinking water.

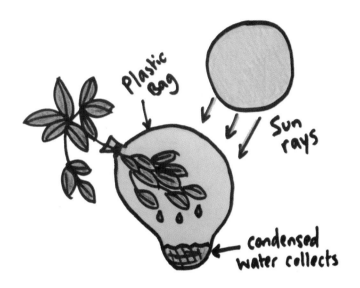

In the early morning, place a small stone in the bottom of the plastic bag and wrap your bag around a bunch of leaves on a tree branch. Make sure the branch that you choose will be in full sun during the day. Tie the top of the bag tightly around the branch and leave it there over the course of the day. Water naturally travels from the trunk of the tree to the leaves, where it transpires into the air. By covering the leaves with the bag, this water will condense in the plastic and collect in the bottom of the bag. You may want to swap branches and leaf bundles as the day progresses to ensure a constant supply. This water doesn't require purifying as that process has already been done by the tree.

DEW DANCING

Before the sun rises, wrap an item of clothing around your legs and walk through an area of long grass covered in drops of dew. Wring out the piece of clothing into your mouth and repeat.

Quick Tips

Water always flows downhill, so lower-lying areas and valleys are good places to look if there are not obvious areas of vegetation.

Insect swarms and popular bird flight paths may also be good indicators of water.

It is crucial for you to remember that any time you drink water without purifying it, you run the risk of becoming sick. If you have any way of purifying the water, do so before consuming it. But if your life depends upon it, and you have no means of purifying available, drink the clearest, most rapidly flowing water you can find very sparingly.

Urban Water

Water is definitely one thing we take for granted in an urban setting. It just comes right out of our taps.

Nothing to it. We may have gotten fussy over the years and now pay more for drinking water than we do for gas, but we all know that in a pinch we can turn on a tap and stave off dehydration.

The average person should consume between sixty-four to 128 ounces of water a day to stay healthy. This means that when a water shortage threatens, you need to have about 128 ounces for each member of your household for each day water is unavailable. Some people choose to store water bottles in their sheds or basements in case an emergency arises. This is one way of ensuring that you have enough to get by.

If you are aware of the possibility of an impending water shortage (you have been warned of a major storm or possible electrical interruption), then fill every available watertight container you can to help you ride through it. Get creative. Your bath, sinks, and even ziplock bags will do. Fill way more than you think you will need. Remember, it's not just for drinking. You will eventually need it for such things as cooking, flushing toilets, and washing.

Conserve as much as you can. Eat foods that require little to no water for their preparation. Only flush the toilet if you have to. Have a sponge bath rather than a full bath. Leave the dirty dishes for a day or so. Obviously, you don't want conditions to become unsanitary, so make sure that if the water shortage drags on, you use what you must to ensure that no one gets sick.

A good source of water can also be a swimming pool. Just because it may be chlorinated doesn't mean that it can't be used for everything else other than consumption.

Dehydration

Dehydration occurs when your body loses more fluids than it consumes. Most people don't consume enough water in their day, and when dehydration symptoms flare up, they misdiagnose them and combat them with diuretics (tea or coffee) and medication that can further exacerbate the problem.

Next time you exhibit any of the follow symptoms, try drinking a big glass of water and waiting for ten minutes to see if it helps.

SYMPTOMS OF MILD DEHYDRATION:

- dry mouth
- fatigue
- thirst
- lack of urination (you should be peeing about once every few hours)
- headache
- dizziness

Water and why we need it . . .

Water makes up about 70 percent of our bodies' composition. It circulates through the blood and is responsible for transporting essential nutrients and oxygen to our organs. It then takes the toxins and waste from those organs and gets them out of our bodies in the forms of sweat and urine. This basically means that if you don't drink enough water, you're not sending good things to your organs and cells, and you're not getting the bad things out of your body. And what does this mean for how you function as a human being? It means that without enough water, you will be sluggish, more prone to sickness, and have less stamina for life.

FYI: Drinking more water can make you look younger. Dehydration of the skin is one of the main causes of wrinkles.

So how much is enough? The most common answer is about sixty-four ounces of water a day. This is pure, filtered water, not soda, coffee, tea, or juice. Anything with caffeine in it (like some energy drinks) actually dehydrates you, and the rule of thumb for that is, for every cup of caffeine, you need to have two cups of water to combat the effect on your body.

If this seems complicated, just start trying to drink more pure water than you currently do. One way of doing this is by filling up a liter bottle that is just for water. Fill it in the morning and challenge yourself to finish it by the end of the day. Your body will thank you. If you manage this easily, then fill it up again. If you manage to make it through two bottles full, you are well on your way to a healthier you.

Caught out on a night out?

When hitting the office turns into hitting the town, no girl wants to look like she's just crawled out from behind her desk. There are a few simple tools to make sure that you always look fresh, fabulous, and ready for anything.

*A small bag of stashed supplies can transform you into Cinderella in no time.

Wear a basic outfit to work that can be easily accessorized. Keep the base layer a fairly neutral color that you can layer over with patterns and brighter colors.

Keep a small bag under your desk with some simple clothing changes in it to spice up your office wear. A pair of killer heels can add sass to your suit. You might lose the jacket in favor of a brightly colored top. A fun belt can help finish off the look.

Add a flashy piece of jewelry—your favorite necklace, some dangly earrings, or a large ring. This is a very effective mood-shifter.

Finally, deepen your makeup tones and add a brighter shade of lipstick.

Weapons

The Great Gun Debate. The first line of defense that most people think about is a gun. Now, I have a real aversion to guns. They scare me and I don't enjoy them. I have heard both sides of the debate, for and against gun ownership, and I am not choosing sides. The bottom line for me is, if you own any type of weapon, you better know how to use it well. If you don't know how to use a weapon, it will probably end up being used against you.

If you are facing someone who knows anything about your weapon of choice, your attacker will know if you know how to use it by the way you hold it and by your confidence in handling it. So if you choose to have a weapon (where the law allows you to), make sure that you have taken the time to become intimately acquainted with it.

If you are prepared to have a gun as your form of protection, make sure that you are mentally prepared to pull the trigger if you have to. Could you kill another human being? The idea of doing it and the reality of doing it are two very different things. If you are not, then it will be taken from you and very likely used against you. So then what is the point of carrying one at all?

For long-term survival situations, guns are a fantastic way of procuring supplies. If you are a good shot and can learn some basic hunting techniques, you will be able to provide yourself and your loved ones with a valuable source of protein from the wild animals around you. You may just have to get the images of Chip and Dale out of your head before aiming for a cute little chipmunk and imagine how good he'll taste after he's cooked.

Knife fighting is the messiest kind of fighting there is. Knives are surprisingly more deadly than guns. If a knife is drawn in a fight, there is a 60 percent chance that one combatant or the other (probably both) will end up with a life-threatening injury or dead. To use a knife, you must already be in close quarters with your attacker, and it is very easy to disarm a knife-wielder if she doesn't know what she is doing. If a knife is your only method of defense, say if you are attacked in a butcher's shop, then use whatever comes in handy to keep yourself safe. Just don't carry one around in your purse as your self-defense weapon of choice or draw one as your first line of defense should you feel slightly nervous.

There are a wide variety of stun guns available on the market, but the basic premise of them all is

that you use them to deliver an electrical charge to your attacker that will disable or immobilize him. Stun guns, although their name suggests otherwise, can kill. So if you choose this weapon, choose it as you would a gun and shoot it with full awareness of the possible consequences. In some states, there are restrictions and bans as far as this weapon is concerned, so if you are crossing borders with it, be aware of these differing laws. Educate yourself and know how to use it well, and keep it in a safe place, away from kids and less responsible adults.

There are some stun guns that shoot out prongs that attach to your assailant, but these require an almost gun-like aim and accuracy to hit your attacker. There are backup features should you miss, but you will lose your element of surprise. It is recommended for women that they purchase a stun gun that delivers a charge on contact. This means that the assailant will be near enough to touch you, and therefore near enough to grab you. If you miss the first time or don't deliver a full charge, you may just make him more mad.

Pepper spray is a pretty good choice of weapon if you feel like you need to carry one. It can be used on an attacker up to ten feet away (depending on the brand). This means that you can maintain your distance and not give your assailant the opportunity to grab you. Because pepper spray does not

cause death to the attacker, people are more likely to use it instantly and without hesitation. This is a good thing. It is easier to wash out of someone's eyes later in apology if you misread the situation. This doesn't mean I want everyone to go around spraying pepper spray on any random stranger who has forgotten his watch and needs to know the time. It just means that your lack of hesitation to use it might save your life.

As with all weapons, pepper spray has its limitations. You need to aim for the assailant's nose and mouth, and it may take a few seconds to become effective. In these few seconds, you may be disarmed and have the pepper spray used against you. The pepper spray is less effective in wind and rain, and there may be some back spray that ends up on you.

Pepper sprays are not usually restricted by law, but please make sure that you research the limitations in your state. Some states have size and type requirements and some do require a permit to carry them.

If you do choose to carry a weapon of some sort, it should never be your first line of defense. Pulling a knife out if some stranger is offering to buy you a drink is never smart. A weapon should be drawn only if all other defensive strategies have failed. I would first try to get away or talk my way out of the situation. Once a weapon is drawn, the hope for a happy outcome for all involved decreases rapidly.

If you are caught in a survival situation where the predators you may encounter are of the animal variety, it's a really good idea to fashion some kind of weapon for defense. My weapon of choice in that situation would be a strong, sharpened stick or a heavy club. I would carry it with me during the day if I were traveling and have it by my side at night.

Educate yourself about the animal predators in your country, and if you are going into the outdoors in a foreign country, educate yourself about the likely predators there. Learn what they look like, how to avoid them, and the best way to deter an attack. It's different for all large predators. For example, you would make noise to scare away a black bear or a lion but play dead to deter a grizzly attack. You would dodge out of the way at the last minute from an attacking

Photo credit: Teren Oddo

Remember, the best weapon that you carry with you into all situations is your mind!

hippo (they aren't very agile and have trouble with quick direction changes). Learn the difference between each. It could save your life.

Car emergency kit

One interesting thing I have noticed about the emergency kits you can get these days in cars is that no one is ever really sure what they contain. So if you have one in the car, check it out. Acquaint yourself with what someone else has decided you need in case of an emergency.

If you don't have an emergency car kit but think that it sounds like a great idea, you can also make one yourself. All you need is a sturdy nylon bag with some or all of the following items in it:

- a two-liter bottle of water
- a first aid kit
- a fire extinguisher
- a warm blanket
- jumper cables
- car oil
- radiator fluid or coolant
- protein bars

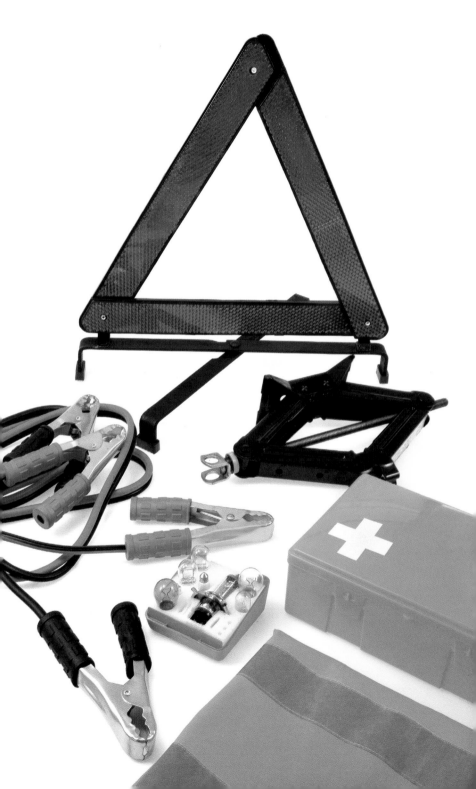

Make sure you know how to use everything in your kit before an emergency arises. It's no use trying to read the instructions when seconds can count.

- a flashlight
- a lighter or waterproof matches
- a multi-tool pocketknife
- a collapsible shovel (in case you get stuck in the mud)
- duct tape

You can add whatever you like that makes you feel safer to your emergency car kit. Some other suggestions are flares and snow chains (if you live in or travel through very cold areas).

Always have some kind of a first aid kit in your vehicle. I have used the first aid kit I keep in the car for everything from being first at the scene of an accident, to blisters from my expensive five-inch heels.

Fire equals life

Fire allows you to boil water you find to make it drinkable if you don't have any other means of filtering it. Fire will cook your food to make it more palatable, help keep large predators at bay, signal for help, and stop you from freezing to death at night. It is one of the essentials that may make the difference between surviving or not.

The one thing that animals fear is fire. With the exception of the fire-fighting rhinoceros in Africa (it's true, look it up), most animals will avoid the heat of a flame. In a survival situation, I would make it a priority to have a fire burning before the sun sets and make sure to have enough wood stock-piled to ensure that the fire burns throughout the night. The fire doesn't need to be a big one. In most cases, simply the smell of the wood burning will be an ample deterrent. Fires are also great for morale. They add a feeling of warmth and safety to a situation that can otherwise feel out of control and scary.

You need three things to make a flame:

1. Oxygen
2. Fuel (something for the fire to catch on to—the drier, the better)
3. A hot enough source to ignite the fuel

In a survival situation, it's always best to keep a fire burning 24/7. This way, you don't have to worry about taking the time to light one every night, and you have a signal ready at any time should a plane fly overhead or a ship pass by your island.

Ways to make a fire

THE FRICTION METHOD

I'm sure that the first thing most people imagine when they think about making a fire in a survival situation is what is called the "friction fire method," or rubbing two sticks together. Now I'm here to tell you that this is far from the best method to get a fire going, particularly if you're in a hurry. It is a very physically demanding and technical process, and I have seen many gifted survivalists not get a fire going after hours of trying this method under pressure. Before embarking on the friction method, try one of the following techniques. They are much simpler and require much less effort.

THE REFRACTION METHOD

One of the easiest methods of making a fire is to allow the sun to shine through material that will magnify the sun's heat.

Human beings have managed to pollute just about every place in the world with their garbage, so you can actually manage to find these types of things in quite remote locations. The most obvious is a piece of glass from such things as a broken bottle or camera lens, but a piece of a plastic bottle will work also. In case you were thinking about leaving it until the last minute, remember, this method will not work at night for obvious reasons.

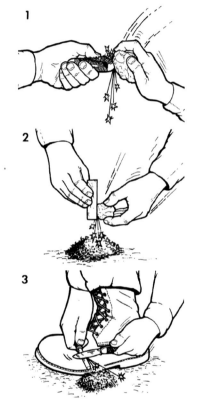

THE FLINT-AND-STEEL METHOD

Another way of making fire is the flint-and-steel method. There is a rock called flint that is found in most places around the world. It tends to be a chalky-looking, fine-grained rock, either light gray or white in color. When struck with steel, such as your pocketknife or a rock with a high metal content, it produces a spark. Aimed just right, this spark can land among your fuel source and catch fire.

If you are unsure about how to identify flint, try a variety of rocks lying around to see if one produces a spark. You have to hit the rock quite hard and sharply to get the spark, but once you get the hang of it, it is an easy and reliable fire-lighting method.

THE BATTERY METHOD

If you are in a more urban environment, a great way of getting a spark is the battery method. This is assuming that you have a flashlight or something that runs on batteries nearby (maybe your camera). You will also need two pieces of wire (perhaps from a nearby fence or the inside of an electrical cord, such as a phone charger).

Attach one wire to the positive end of the battery and one wire to the negative end. When you bring the two wires close together, a spark will jump between them. If you can place your tinder between the wires, you should be able to light it from the spark.

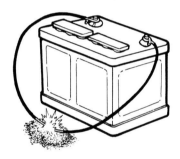

TINDER

Once you have managed to figure out the method that you will use to get a spark, you will need to have a place to put the spark to ignite it into a flame. You probably have a limited amount of tries to get a spark, so make sure you spend time preparing a place to put it before you begin.

Stack a fire with tinder (very small flammable material, such as newspaper or fire-starters) in the middle and then put small twigs on top of that.

The reason for this is that smaller twigs catch fire first, and as they burn, they allow time for larger sticks to catch fire. Larger sticks generally take a little time to catch, and your tinder may burn up before this happens if you have only large twigs on your fire.

If you are in the middle of nowhere, chances are you will not have any man-made material to use for tinder. In this case you will have to create a tinder nest to aim your spark into. A tinder nest is similar to a bird's nest, which has larger material on the outside and finer material on the inside.

You can make your tinder nest out of dried grass, dried cattail heads, thin layers of tree bark, moss, and dead pine needles. To make the outer rim of the nest, it is best to tie a loose overhand knot (like the first knot when tying your shoelace) with shredded bark. This will create a basketlike nest that you can then fill with finer fibers. The smaller and drier your inner layers are, the more likely you will be successful in getting a flame. Make sure that there are no holes in your nest that the spark may fall out of.

Photo credit: Teren Oddo

REFLECTIVE FIRE

When you're on the move in a survival situation, use a reflective fire to keep safe and warm at night. This is less labor intensive than building a shelter and can actually be much warmer.

The key is to find a flat wall surface at least three feet high. Lie between this and a low-burning, body-length fire that you've built a rock wall on the other side of. This is not a good option if you think it may rain (definitely build or seek shelter if this is the case). You must also make sure you have enough wood to last the night, as a 3 a.m. wood collection run is never a good thing.

Running in high heels

Picture if you can a female outdoor guide in hiking boots (me) who does not even own a dress and rarely gets to shower two consecutive days in a row, and then place her on a movie set and into the most glamorous feminine outfits money can buy. Then ask her to run, leap, and fight in them.

When I started out as a stuntwoman, I didn't even own a pair of shoes with heels. Suddenly I was being squeezed into a pair of six-inch Jimmy Choos. Even basic moves such as standing up and walking were difficult. Who'd have thought putting one foot in front of the other could cause such distress?

My learning curve was steep and fast; no one wants to employ a stunt performer whose idea of a challenge is walking in the shoes the costume department supplies. And no actress wants a stunt double who makes her look like an old, arthritic cowboy from behind. Thank goodness for a dancer friend of mine who set me straight. "Stay on your toes" was what she said to me, and suddenly I could run, fight, and leap like a superhero in the tallest of heels.

So that's my tip to you, but with some refinements.

On flat ground where you can move at a slower pace, it's okay to place the heel of the shoe down before the toe when you're running. On uneven ground or steps, or when you're running for your life (or the bus), you should run on your toes. It may take some practice, but it's a really good calf workout, and once you've mastered this technique, you will get where you need to go fast, and look graceful too.

I had to learn from scratch, so if you are new to heels, I recommend practicing in them as much as you can. I've vacuumed in them, made my dinner in them, and gone grocery shopping in them (and sweatpants!) until I could walk gracefully onto the set and out to dinner. Embrace the feminine and sexy you, but be ready to kick ass in them if you need to.

If you do find yourself running for your life in high heels, get rid of them and hit the pavement barefoot. You can still run with cuts and bruises on your feet, but a twisted ankle from falling off the heels will stop you in your tracks. If you are running for the train or bus in heels, remember to run on your toes. This will give you extra speed and dexterity as well as help you avoid a twisted ankle.

If you have twisted your ankle and are far from help, your best bet is to keep your shoe on and keep moving. If you can still hold up your weight, strap something around your shoe to give it support, find a stick to lean on, and get out of the situation as soon as possible. Removing the shoe will result in increased swelling and make it harder to start walking when you do need to move. If you are in a safe place and don't need to move, then rest, ice, compress, and elevate as soon as possible.

CATWOMAN DEFEATS SIX-INCH HEELS

My favorite heels story happened during one of my first big stunt jobs. I was one of the doubles for Sharon Stone on *Catwoman,* and I had to be kicked across the room by said superhero and thrown into a big, framed photo of Sharon in such a way that I shattered the glass and then landed with my head by the frame and my heels away from it. If any of you have had the misfortune of being tossed through the air, you know that everything happens very quickly and you usually just end up where you end up. But this sequence had to happen in a certain way in order to make the action match the acting. Needless to say, I had a lot on my mind.

At the last moment, the costumer came up to me with the shoes I was supposed to wear and said, "Please be careful not to scratch these. They are handmade by a designer in Italy and had to be shipped over especially for the filming. We have only two pairs and they are $8,000 each." No pressure!

The director yelled, "Action!" and I have to confess, there were way more pressing things on my mind than those designer shoes. I had to hit my mark the same second Halle Berry kicked out. The wire I was attached to had to be taut before I got launched backward so I wouldn't break my ribs. My chin had to be tucked in such a way that I didn't go headfirst into the frame and break my neck. I had to hit the glass with the points of both my elbows and my butt so that it would shatter, then keep my eyes closed so that I didn't get glass in them. I had to keep my face away from the three cameras so that I wouldn't be recognized. And finally, I had to land in just the right way. Everything went so fast, but when the director called, "Cut!" everyone cheered. Everything had gone as planned. Everything, that is, except for the fact that I had managed to sever the heel of my left shoe completely. I sheepishly looked toward the costumer. As I suspected, she was the only one not cheering.

We then did a second take for more angles and I broke the left heel off the spare pair too . . . Duct tape, anyone?

Knots

Grandma had the right idea. Your knitting knots may be the very thing to help you make a secure shelter that will assist you in surviving a storm. Learning to tie a few knots is a very useful skill to have up your sleeve for all manner of situations.

My favorite knot is the reef knot. It is a very secure knot that is easily untied. When tying a reef knot, take two ropes and cross them to form a half knot. Cross them a second time in the opposite direction and pull the ends tightly. This knot is also really useful for tying the ends of a broken lace together to enable you to tie your shoes up until you can get to the store to buy a new lace.

The only other knot I really use is a version of the trucker's hitch. Tie a loop in one end of a

*"When you don't know knots, tie lots." Knots don't need to be fancy, they just need to work. No one will be judging you on your knot-tying when they rescue you. Do whatever you can to make things safe and secure.

rope (any way you like), and then feed the other end of the rope through the loop and pull down hard, tying this loose end off with a couple of half hitches.

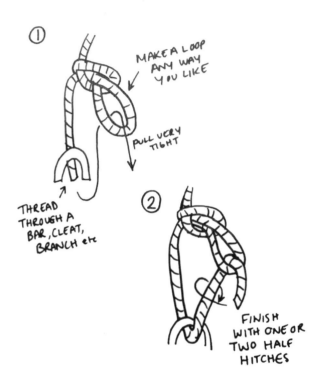

① MAKE A LOOP ANY WAY YOU LIKE

PULL VERY TIGHT

THREAD THROUGH A BAR, CLEAT, BRANCH etc

② FINISH WITH ONE OR TWO HALF HITCHES

Food at camp

Having a case of middle-of-the-night munchies? While a fire will usually scare critters away from your camp, it is also a good idea to make sure that you aren't doing anything to attract them back.

Any food preparation, especially of meat, should be done away from where you plan to sleep. You should also store your food away from your sleeping area and make sure you wash any food

smells off your hands and face before heading to bed for the night.

The bonus of a survival situation, if you can look at it that way, is that you are probably existing off food that the larger carnivores can get themselves out in the wilderness, so the chances of them wandering into your camp for that is unlikely. However, if you did manage to catch an amazing trout by hand, make sure that the bear doesn't think that it is you who smells so fishy-sweet in the middle of the night!

And it's not just the bigger creatures that can cause damage. People laugh at me when I say that we have to put all the nice-smelling stuff away in case of mice, but let me tell you, mice can really ruin a trip. A couple of times I have had clients who haven't done a thorough search of their bags and have left a food wrapper way down deep in their packs for the night. Mice will eat a hole through anything to get to that amazing-smelling treat. These clients had mouse-sized holes in their tent, in their backpacks, and in almost every piece of their clothing. It cost them more than a thousand dollars to replace their gear. All because of one little chocolate bar wrapper. But at least it wasn't a bear, because he might have eaten more than just a hole in the tent to get to that wrapper!

Creatures of the night

When you're traveling, or under unusual circumstances, never go anywhere alone at night. Unless you're in a desert survival situation that would require you to travel at night to avoid the scorching heat of the day, I always recommend finding a safe place before dark and staying there until light. Nighttime is more dangerous in terms of predators (of both the human and animal variety), and it is easy to lose your way or have an accident when you can't see very well.

Sound boring? Well, lucky for me, I am an outdoors adventure girl, so most things I want to do are day activities. I get up at first light and head out and run myself ragged, so by the time the sun sets, I'm ready to find a nice resting place for the night.

Cautious trust

Don't trust anyone you don't know. It may seem kind of sad, but, hey, I've never been mugged. And don't think that because you have spent a day hanging out with someone, you know that person.

Now, I'm not saying don't hang out with strangers, because getting to know people is one of the joys of traveling to new places. I'm just saying don't ask them to hold your purse while you go to the bathroom.

Carry a city survival kit

Use a cute little zip bag to hold the following items:

- tampons
- a couple of painkillers
- a small tube of superglue (to stick on that high heel if it breaks off on the way to a meeting)
- some gum or mints
- an energy bar
- lip balm
- a couple of bandages (for those new-shoe blisters)

You can get creative and fill it with the things that matter most to you. Just remember to keep it well stocked.

Last-minute essentials

My trip essentials list is very short. These are the things that I check that I have as I walk out the door. You might want to make your list a little longer, but this is mine:

- credit card
- passport
- phone

- travel details
- prescription medication (if applicable)

All other things I know that I can either live without or buy with my credit card. Of course, forgetting things is not ideal nor is spending money on items I already own, but if I forget the above things, my time away might become problematic, whereas all else is a mere inconvenience.

Then there are my last-minute necessities. This is the list of things that I may not *need* but that make my trip away much more pleasant. Your list may look different. I suggest taking a minute to write down the things you'd like to have with you when you travel.

Once you've made your list, put it with your suitcase. That way, when you're hitting the road, you can simply pull out the list and cross off your necessities as you add them to your bag. This will make sure you don't forget anything as you are rushing around throwing things into your bag.

Something like this would work:

- yoga mat
- iPod speakers
- converter plugs
- bandages
- vitamins
- sunscreen

Of course, you can always leave off the items that aren't relevant to that particular trip (like woolen mittens for your trip to the Bahamas), but a list will prevent you from leaving anything important behind.

Use the sky

Left your watch behind and your phone is out of juice? If you can see the sun, and you can see the horizon, and you know roughly what time the sun sets (okay, so that's a lot of factors), you can figure out what time it is. Hold three fingers parallel to the horizon. Each stack of three fingers between the sun and the horizon is roughly an hour of time.

Which way is up?

There are many ways to figure out the direction you're facing when a compass is nowhere in sight. The problem is that it becomes quite complicated depending on which side of the equator you're on. Once you have crossed that line, all the rules that you learned for one side of the earth need to be reversed for the other side—except for this one: the sun rises in the east and sets in the west. Just think of it as "Ew!"

Night navigation

As I've said previously, I always advise people not to move at night unless it is really necessary. Chances are you will not have a light to see by and this will make walking quite difficult. You risk physical harm, and in a survival situation your physical capability may make the difference between your making it out or not.

Some situations that make night movement necessary are if you are in a desert and the heat is too extreme to travel during the day, or if you are being pursued by someone who will find you if you travel in daylight.

If you are forced to move at night, here are the most basic navigational guides to keep you walking in the right direction.

THE STARS

Some people, when they are navigating at night, pick a particularly bright star and orient themselves by it. The problem with this is that all stars move through the sky in different orbit motions, kind of like this:

Stars don't follow the sun and moon's east-west track. So you will end up going in a different direction at the end of the night than what you aimed for at the start.

The only star that doesn't follow this kind of pattern is the North Star. But it's visible only in the Northern Hemisphere. The Southern Hemisphere star compass guide is related to perhaps one of the most famous constellations, the Southern Cross.

Southern Hemisphere navigation by the stars

For this you will need to find the Southern Cross. It is a very easy constellation to find. In order to

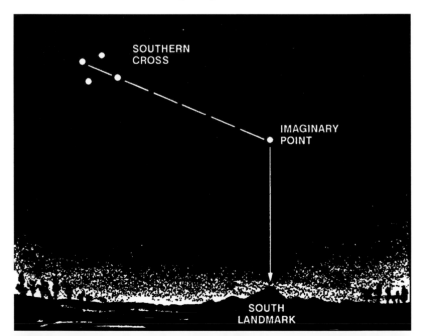

distinguish it from other cross shapes in the sky, look for the two bright "pointer" stars located next to it.

In order to find south you need to draw an imaginary line through the longest length of the cross, intersecting the top and bottom stars. Then draw a perpendicular bisector (a ninety-degree intersecting line) through the line you created between the two pointer stars. The place that these two lines intersect should indicate a southern direction.

You will be able to figure out the other directions once you have found south. For example, if you need to travel in a westerly direction, keep this point on your left-hand side as you travel.

It is a good idea to practice this skill each time you spy the cross and pointers in the sky so you can be proficient if you ever have to use it.

Northern Hemisphere navigation by the stars

Locating the North Star is a little tricky, as it is not one of the brightest stars in the sky. Luckily, it has two constellations nearby that are fairly easy to identify. The first is the Big Dipper, which is part of the constellation Ursa Major. It looks kind of like a saucepan. The second is Cassiopeia, which looks like a large W.

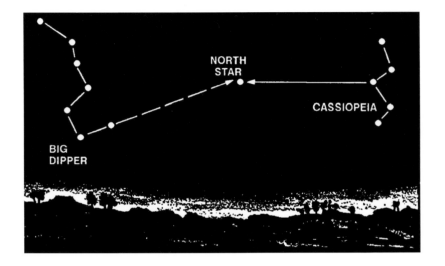

The first thing to do is follow the edge of the Big Dipper's cup, farthest from the handle of the "saucepan," five times its length along to find a medium-bright star. This is the North Star, which sits in a northerly direction. To double-check that you have the right one, locate Cassiopeia. The North Star should sit halfway between the Big Dipper and Cassiopeia.

THE MOON

The moon follows a similar arc in the sky as the sun. It rises in the east and sets in the west. So if you happen to be fortunate enough to have a moonlit night to travel by, this is a good place to start.

The thing with the moon, however, is that it travels at a different speed than the sun. We have all seen the moon out during the day, which means it is not out during those nights. On nights with no moon, you will have to rely on the stars to guide you.

Chapter 3

BE ADAPTABLE

Stop, look, and listen

In an unexpected situation, if your life is not in immediate danger, which will be the case more often than not, stop, look, and listen. From my many years as an outdoor survival expert and stuntwoman, I've had this response so ingrained in me that it actually now overrules my fight-or-flight mechanism. The first thing I do when something seems unusual is to stop. This unusual something could be a noise in the bushes, something crawling on my skin, or something that catches my sight out of the corner of my eye. I then look and listen. Does it happen again?

If it is something crawling on my skin, how big does it feel? How fast is it moving? Is it similar to something I have felt before? Most bugs in the outdoors, even the poisonous ones, will not bite or sting unless they feel threatened. Most people get stung or bitten when they try to get the creepy crawly thing off. You should first discern what it is and then try to remove it without causing yourself or the creature any harm. In most cases, a short, sharp flick of the fingers works well.

If you learn to make stop, look, and listen your first response, rather than react in panic, you are taking an important step to ensuring your survival.

Is it something bigger, like a large animal moving through the bush? Is the sound coming closer or going away? Is this a sound that you usually hear around your home at night? If not, what does it sound like? A gate being shut by hand or merely swinging in the wind?

There are so many scenarios here that I cannot possibly cover them all, but I'm sure you get the idea.

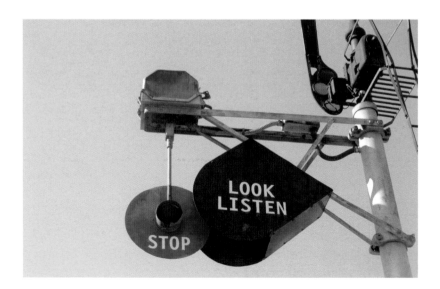

The fight-or-flight response

All animals have an instinctive response to threats in which the sympathetic nervous system discharges and fills the body with catecholamine hormones, the most common of which is adrenaline. This surge of adrenaline is a survival response that gives you a burst of energy so that you can get away from the threat. We see this in wildlife documentaries when a not-so-agile wildebeest has a huge spurt of almost inconceivable energy and manages to get away from the lion chasing it.

Humans are no different. The fight-or-flight response was really effective back when humans were faced with threats such as saber-toothed tigers and angry woolly mammoths, but it's not as effective today because we are rarely faced with life-threatening situations.

More often than not, our fight-or-flight response fires off when someone almost opens a door in our face or honks a horn at us when we are standing on the side of the road. You will know that this response has happened because you will have such body reactions as sweaty armpits, shallow, rapid breathing, elevated heart rate, and all-over trembling.

If your life is in immediate danger, then capitalize on the short burst of adrenaline that the fight-or-flight response provides and get out of harm's way. I have never run so fast in my life as I did when a flaming car went in an unexpected direction on the set of *X-Men: The Last Stand* and tumbled toward me end over end. I'm sure I would have won an Olympic gold medal for the time it took me to dash ten meters to safety behind the concrete barriers. Even Hugh Jackman agreed it was a very near miss and toasted my successful escape with a raise of his cigar, saying, "Shit, hey, that was close."

The fight-or-flight response allows your body to take over your brain for a moment and triggers a purely physical reaction. It can end up turning into something akin to panic. Panic can be your deadliest enemy. It is the response that sends you off into the darkness in the middle of the night without a flashlight as you try to flee from a random noise by your camp, or it can make you force your beloved partner into oncoming traffic when you see a skunk wandering down the footpath toward you (true story).

It may come down to just you

No one likes to think that she has to do everything herself. It's also not encouraging to think that no one will come and rescue you if you are lost. But in a survival situation, you need to begin to mentally prepare yourself for the idea that you may have to assist in your own recovery.

I was once in charge of a group of kids who were sailing when a massive storm came through and knocked their boat over. I needed help preventing the boat from sinking after I had rescued all the kids and had patched a radio call through to our safety officer. The kids were terrified and the storm was really kicking up, so I entertained them

Nothing brings on panic faster than an idle mind. But knowing that you are working toward ensuring your own health and well-being will do wonders for your mental state.

by showing them how the signal mirror worked. This ended up being the only reason the safety officer found us as we drifted from the original coordinates. The kids calmed down, and we assisted in our own recovery.

From the second you realize that things are looking grim, begin to do what *you* can to assist in your survival and make your situation better. Not only will this increase your chances of making it out alive, but it will also enable you to be in better condition when you finally do get out.

Don't wait until it gets dark before trying to secure somewhere warm and safe for the night. Shelters take time to construct, and without matches, making a fire can take hours. Plan ahead. Find water if you can before you get thirsty. Sitting down, doing nothing, and waiting for someone to find you is a good strategy if you are lost in the mall, but it will work only if someone finds you before dark in the outdoors. (Note: I'm not telling you to travel from your last known destination. I'm just asking you to be active within that area.)

First assessment

In any unexpected situation, the first thing to do is to assess it. Consider your strengths and weaknesses within the scenario and find a way to make the strengths work for you and to leave the weaknesses by the wayside.

And I'm not just talking about out in the wilderness. Unexpected situations can occur in the workplace every day—things like last-minute strategy changes to important projects, emergency meetings, surprise firings and hierarchy changes, and funding cuts. All of these things can send you

When the world is falling down around your ears, it really is best to think about your strengths and what you can do well. Spending time worrying about the attributes you don't have or the things you can't do is a waste of time and energy.

into a tailspin. In every case, assess the situation, look at your strengths and weaknesses, and make your strengths work for you. You might be surprised at how empowering this is and how amazing the results can be. At the very least, no matter the outcome, you will feel like you tackled the situation the best way you could.

Planning

Always, always, always make a plan. By weighing the pros and cons of whatever situation you are in, you should be able to find the best course of action. By making a plan, you will avoid wasting time and energy trying avenues of action that will not be effective. It may seem that taking the time to make a plan delays action and therefore prolongs an outcome. This may be the case sometimes (like when you need to move fast to avoid an oncoming obstacle), but usually, sitting down and making a plan saves time in the long run.

By making a plan, you will feel proactive. In a survival situation, a feeling of helplessness can be just as deadly as the environment you are in.

Your plan should assess the seriousness of the situation that you are in. Was it an earthquake that shook your house for a few minutes? Did your fight-or-flight mechanism take you to the

Pros	Cons

street, where you joined your neighbors for a quick chat before returning home, straightening the pictures, and making sure all was okay? Was it a hurricane that left you without power and cut you off from your nearest town for three days? In this case, you would need to think about how to keep yourself warm, hydrated, and fed until power could be restored.

Your plan should take into consideration your "personal toolbox." This is comprised of the things that you have learned throughout life. The more education that you bring to the situation, the better the outcome.

Here are some things that could be considered part of your personal toolbox:

- What kinds of knots do you know how to tie?
- Can you read a road map instead of relying on the GPS?
- Are you excellent at calming and entertaining children?
- Have you taken a first aid course? (You will be amazed at what you remember from that life-saving course you took as a teenager.)

Say this five times fast: Proper planning prevents poor performance.

• Can you whip up a meal out of almost anything?

You never know what may come in handy in any given situation, so count every skill as a possible bonus.

Although I've been a stuntwoman for ten years, I was an outdoor guide before that. This meant that when a director suddenly decided he wanted three wire-based stunts instead of two, and he wanted to shoot them before dark, I could dive in and use my rope knowledge to rig the stunts and help get them all shot before dark. This prevented the inevitable panic and chaos that would have usually accompanied this scenario. It also saved the production the hundreds of thousands of dollars it would have cost to get everyone back the next day.

Reaction process

It is important to remember that even though you have made a plan, it does not have to be set in stone. If it is not working for you, or the situation changes for some reason, reassess and make a new plan. Don't stubbornly persist with a plan that doesn't work.

Here is the tricky part: I can't tell you what to plan. There are more possible scenarios of what life

may throw your way than there are people on the planet. All I can do is tell you that by slowing down and making a plan, you are more likely to live to tell your tale than someone who runs off in a blind panic through the woods.

Change

I love the Serenity Prayer. Keeping in mind that there are a lot of different faiths out there, I've modified it slightly to make it more accessible to everyone:

Give me the serenity to accept the things
  I cannot change,
The courage to change the things I can,
And the wisdom to know the difference.

There are things that happen to us that we cannot prevent or change. There will be moments when you have to get from point A to point B. This fact is inevitable. It must happen for whatever reason. The only thing that you can change is how you choose to do this. You can get angry and hate the fact that you have to get from point A to point B, or you can accept it and make the most of it. The only person who is really in charge of how much you enjoy the experience is you.

Deming's quote below makes me laugh because it's so true. Some people so stubbornly stick to a way of being that they take themselves out of being. It is your ability to adapt and change that will help you survive. For example, when it gets hot, do you find ways to cool down by perhaps traveling or

"It's not necessary to change. Survival is not mandatory."
—W. Edwards Deming

working at night? Or do you persist with what you are doing until heatstroke strikes you down?

Many people persist with situations that are not working for them well beyond the time that most people would seek to change the situation. Are you one of them? Are you stubbornly sticking to something that is compromising your life's happiness? Is it time for a change?

Think before you act

Believe me, I have taken some silly risks and gotten away with doing it. Of course, what is adventure without risk? I do, however, like to think that the risks I took were calculated and based on that hard-to-quantify sense we call "intuition." If I had a bad feeling about something, I wouldn't take the risk no matter how harmless it seemed.

You might imagine that most stunt performers think before they act, but the reality is that we are expected to just do the stunts without asking a lot of questions. Some of the best stunt performers are those who don't think too carefully about what they are going to do before they do it. Coincidentally, they are also the ones who have the best emergency room stories.

I pride myself for having a stunt career that has lasted ten years and has involved very few major injuries. And this is not because I don't take risks. I just reduce the number of risks I take. Before doing a stunt, I take charge of my own safety and check out every element of the stunt and the environment around me. Quite often I will find nails or glass that I may have landed on had I not known they were there. If something is too risky, I come up with a plan that still delivers the stunt the director wants but doesn't put my life at risk.

A good example of this occurred once when I thought I was going to have an easy day at work. But when I got on the set, it had been decided that my character was going to be knocked off the upper deck of a ferry by a crane and tossed forty feet into the water below.

This was all right with me. A bigger day than I had planned, sure, but what a cool stunt! I didn't get to check out the rig until I was up on the deck of the boat and we were already out in the bay. The production crew wanted me to just dive right into the stunt, but I saw that the railing was quite high and that I might have trouble clearing it. I also wanted to see how fast the arm of the crane would swing so that I could time my leap. I knew this was the kind of stunt that I would want to do only once.

As I watched the arm swing, I realized that there would be no space for my legs to clear the railing once the crane hit me. I would be sandwiched between the heavy crane and the metal railing. A very ugly scenario. After a few minutes of chatting with the riggers, we came up with a great solution. The stunt went off like a charm and everyone was happy. If I hadn't taken a moment to think the stunt through, I would have ended up in the emergency room, and the shot would have been ruined.

Check for yourself

The "experts" around you may not have all the answers either. Don't just assume that because people tell you they can do something well, this means that they really can. Check over the situation and the proposed solution, and don't be afraid to ask questions. The expert in charge may have a lot on his or her mind and may have overlooked a potential problem.

As a stuntwoman I am often attached to wires for gravity-defying stunts. The stunt riggers and coordinators are responsible for anchoring the wires and attaching them to my body. I am responsible merely for getting my body into the required positions to make the stunt match the director's vision.

I was once lined up to do a stunt with a wire wrapped between my legs and over my shoulder. The aim was to shoot a scene in which another character's uppercut would send me in a backward somersault and land me on my stomach at the base of a tree. I was minutes away from doing the stunt, when I decided to do what I always do—check the rigging. This wasn't because I distrusted the riggers, but just because it is part of how I manage the risks I take. The person responsible for setting the anchors had mixed up the stunt sequences and placed my anchor in the wrong spot. At first I didn't want to speak up because I thought that maybe I had it wrong in my head, but finally, I took the rigger aside and asked him quietly about the anchor point. Turns out it *was* in the wrong place. Had I not said anything, I would have been pulled headfirst into the ground. Hard. It would have probably broken my neck. My awareness of the environment around me and my instinct to ask questions saved my life.

Use your head

No matter what, there will always be a man who, without much training, is stronger than I am. They are genetically built that way. Yes, there are some very strong women out there who could beat Indiana Jones in an arm-wrestling contest, but in general, men are physically stronger than women. I'll give them that. So how do I keep up?

I use my head. I find that I am very good at coming up with alternatives to brute force. It's as simple as that. We invented tools for a reason. They make our lives simpler. In a survival situation that requires more muscle than I have, I sit down for a minute and find a simpler way of doing something.

If I need to move a heavy rock, for instance, I roll it rather than lift or try to carry it. If I need to move a heavy object, I find that a pry bar works better than throwing my back out by trying to use

my arms and knees. I actually failed physics in high school, so I am the worst person to say this, but it is all a matter of physics. Pulley systems, levers, and fulcrums are all ways to move heavy objects without relying on brute strength.

It's also important to know when to move on and try something different. There may be another rock that is easier to move and will suit your needs just fine. Perhaps get three people to move it instead of just you. There are always ways around using brute strength, and sometimes those alternatives work even better in the end.

Risks

Women in general have an aversion to risk. In other words, they like to play it safe. This is a fantastic survival trait.

I don't know if you have spent much time observing animals, but this is the trait that keeps them alive. Take the gopher, for example. In many a wildlife documentary, we see the little gopher poke its head out and then quickly pop it back in. Next time, it sticks its head out a little farther. The gopher is slowly testing the air, checking out the situation, and seeing if there is danger lurking around. Finally, if the coast is clear, it will come out and happily forage or play. This is the way the gopher population survives.

In an unpredictable situation you will need to constantly weigh the risks of every action. Jumping from rock to rock may be a fun activity, but in a survival situation, a twisted ankle could mean not being mobile enough to get to water supplies—and we know what happens when you can't get water.

So it seems to me that being a little bit averse to risk is a huge advantage in a survival situation. I'm not saying take no risks, because there will be times when you will need to. I'm just saying that recognizing risks, and doing your best to minimize them is a great strategy.

Wants and needs

Take a couple of minutes to look at your life and think about the difference between your wants and your needs. A need is something that you will not survive without. You might be thinking right now about your favorite coffeemaker or hair curler, but the bottom line is that unless you will physically die without it, you don't *need* it.

Use your voice

Women are less likely to engage in physical battles than men are. They are more likely to try to talk their way around an argument and negotiate. Although this might drive a husband or

boyfriend mad in an everyday scenario, it may just save everyone's life in a survival situation. The last thing that a group of people in a survival situation needs is to turn on each other physically. There is enough stuff trying to kill you out there without members of your own group adding to the fight.

This is also a handy skill to have on your side in the boardroom when all negotiations have screeched to a halt and tempers are flying.Use your communication skills to calm the situation and come up with an alternative that works for everyone.

It is also possible to talk your way out of a potentially violent situation. I'm not a trained negotiator, so I can't tell you exactly what you should do, but I will say that you should try to read the situation and figure out how to diffuse it with words, even if you don't mean them. It is way better to lie a little in these situations and walk away unharmed. If you find yourself in a life-threatening situation, it's not losing face to accept blame and try to walk away.

Adapt to the situation

It's good to know when to stop trying something that is no longer working for you. An example of this in a survival setting may be trying to move a heavy boulder in order to flatten out a sleeping area. It's not giving up to stop moving the boulder and find another place to sleep if continuing to try to move the boulder wastes precious energy.

I believe this is relevant in everyday life as well. How many of you think that running is the best way to stay fit? Yet when you do it your knees ache, your back hurts, you get shin splints, and you feel exhausted for days. Running doesn't work for everyone, so don't keep persisting until you end up in a hospital getting your ligaments repaired. Try cycling or another exercise activity instead.

Those of us in the stunt industry often end up working for a variety of bosses. Our bosses in this case are the stunt coordinators. They are the ones who work out how the performers can achieve the director's vision. They are usually the ones who hire us and therefore can fire us too.

Much like bosses in the business world, every stunt coordinator is different and has a different way of doing things. Unlike the business world, however, I might have a different boss every day. This means that my way of conducting myself at work has to be different every day. Some stunt coordinators want you to work closely with the actors and others don't even want you to talk to them. There are ones who love your input and ones who will fire you for speaking up when you have an idea. The problem is, unless you have worked for a coordinator before, you have no idea how to conduct yourself. If you don't learn to adapt to

*Changing something that is making a situation worse is not giving up. It's being smart.

his style—and quickly—you may never work for that person (or his coordinator friends) again. Talk about pressure!

I have found a way of functioning within this system that allows me to still be myself and maintain my integrity yet also ensure that I get hired again. I usually ask my friends in the business about a coordinator before I get to the set so I know something of how he likes to work. I never take anything for granted. The coordinator is my boss, so if I am asked to step in and choreograph a few moves by the director, I will find the coordinator and clear it with him first. The main thing is that I remain flexible.

Just to be clear, I am not telling you this story to suggest that you should compromise who you are as a person. I have been asked to do a few things that I was not comfortable with and that I felt compromised my integrity. I was once asked to get naked to rehearse a stunt that I would be naked for. There was absolutely no reason to rehearse naked, as it wasn't an integral part of the sequence. I refused and I lost the job. I never worked for that coordinator again, but I am okay with that. Being flexible is different than breaking your own rules, and only you will know the difference. But adapting to survive in the workplace is essential. It will feel more like going with the flow than fighting upstream, and who doesn't want a conflict-free workplace?

Chapter 4
EDUCATE YOURSELF

Knowledge is empowerment

There is an old Latin saying that goes *"scientia potentia est."* It means "knowledge is power." I prefer to think of it as knowledge is *empowerment*. When I gather skills and am confident that I know what to do in a given situation, I feel empowered.

What you don't know could kill you. In everyday life, not knowing the answer to a question will probably result in something as simple as a B on an exam rather than an A, or another trip around the block while you search for the restaurant where you're meeting your friends. While these things may seem traumatic at the time, in a survival situation, not knowing something and continuing your course of action anyway could result in injury or death.

Learn new skills

Learning new skills is always a good idea. Not only can they prove useful in an unexpected situation, but they can also keep your mind and body active.

Stretching yourself is the best way to improve yourself.

I learn by doing, and I learn best when I have a teacher. There are many good teachers and courses out in the world today ready to impart their knowledge on a whole range of subjects. Look for them online, in the phone book, or in the newspaper.

There are lots of people who claim to be experts at something, so be careful of whom you choose to be your mentor. I suggest going with a reputable company or someone who has good

"star" rating rather than just the cheapest price. I do believe that you get what you pay for.

Practice skills that you have learned. This way, when everything is going wrong, you are far more likely to remember what to do, having tried it before. It is also better to make those learning mistakes when your life or reputation doesn't depend on it.

Learn first aid

Take a first aid course, or at the very least a CPR course, and then update it every two years. I have taken four weeklong wilderness first aid courses. This means that when I head out into the bush with a group of people for whom I am responsible, my concern for the physical safety of those around me is at a minimum. This means that I can enjoy the experience a hell of a lot more. Sure, I am still looking out for things that could go wrong, but I am not worried about what to do if something does go wrong. I am prepared.

I will never forget how helpless and shook up my mother felt one day at a playground when a child fell off a piece of play equipment and stopped breathing right in front of her. Fortunately, someone else with first aid experience intervened. Otherwise, the situation might have ended in tragedy.

My mom signed up for a first aid course the very next weekend. I really feel that learning basic first aid is just another way of letting your family know you love them enough to want to look after them the best you can.

Education leads to power (of body, mind, and attitude)

I recommend taking some kind of self-defense course. You will feel great and more positive about your abilities to deal with any situation. But

The more I learn, the more I realize that my first teacher had it right—it's better to run than fight.

remember that this doesn't mean that you will have enough skills to pick a fight with the nearest bar-brawling bully. I have been trained to use all kinds of weapons and martial arts forms for more than seventeen years. The more I learn, the more I realize that if a stronger person has me pinned, even if he doesn't have fight training, he generally has the upper hand.

When I was a teenager, I thought I was pretty tough and believed that if it came down to it, I could fight back and always win. I was fortunate when I started learning martial arts to have a really smart teacher. He was an Ultimate Fighter (a master of many different disciplines) and also an Olympic-level sprinter. He told me that if he ever had to choose between fighting and running, he would always run. He chose not to look at it as running away from something but as running toward a smarter choice. And this guy fought for a living!

Tactics under attack

Don't let an attacker get near enough to grab you. When Ultimate Fighting first became a popular sport, the winners were generally fighters who had a high level of wrestling skills. Any form of grappling or wrestling will subdue someone quite quickly, so it's best if you can avoid getting into a position that involves a struggle of basic strength. Keep something in between you and your attacker until you can get the attention of someone who can help you or you can find an opportunity to run away.

The best form of physical defense for a woman comes from the element of surprise. You will be underestimated only once, so choose your moment wisely. Most "grab and run" attacks happen in public areas. The attacker won't rape or harm a woman there. He will put her in a vehicle or move her somewhere else where no one will interrupt. The first few seconds of the attack usually occur in the most public place you're likely to be. This means that if you manage to break free, you have a better chance of getting help. The longer that you wait, the more likely you will be taken somewhere far away, where no one will hear you scream.

The thing to remember when using the element of surprise is that your attacker already thinks that you are weaker than he is or else he would not have attacked you in the first place. Use this assumption against him. Allow him to think that you are defenseless and that you have been cowed by him, and when he has dropped his guard, make your move.

The move that I would discourage most is trying to punch your assailant. I don't know about your hands, but mine (and most women's) are quite small and would break easily if I struck another human's bones. We are just not built for bare-knuckle boxing. If you are going for a hit, use the heel of your hand and aim for a soft part of your assailant's face, ideally the nose. He is going to be watching for a kick to his most vulnerable parts (between his legs), but will probably not be expecting the heel of your hand to hit the bridge of his nose. Breaking his nose will cause him excruciating pain and make his eyes water, which will give you a chance to break free.

A karate chop (with the side of your hand) to his throat will damage his windpipe and restrict airflow, thereby giving him something way more pressing to think about than holding you down. Just remember, you will probably get only one chance to surprise him, so wait for the right moment and give it all you've got.

In a threatening situation, use your head. Sometimes the best weapons are things that are not traditionally thought of as weapons. Not wanting to show my age, I'd say, "MacGyver it." (Look him up online, kids. He is my hero.) Some of my favorite examples are keys and pens. Both are sharp enough to hurt someone so that you can get some space between you and your attacker.

There is a moment in every attack when the predator does something stupid and the prey has an opportunity to get away. If he gets his head near yours, hit his nose with your forehead as hard as you can. Breaking his nose may give you precious moments to get away. And if you find a really good hiding spot, just stay there. He will give up looking eventually.

Heed advice

Avoid areas that you have heard are dangerous. Why take a chance if someone else has had trouble there?

I remember when I was traveling through Africa with my best friend, we met this girl who had stitches in her hand and side. We asked what had happened, and she said that she had taken a short-cut through a cornfield and was stabbed by natives during an attempted robbery. We happened to pass that same cornfield and noticed there were warning signs posted all along it. I asked the girl why she had done it anyway, and she said that she thought nothing would happen to her. Well, she almost died.

Of course, there is always an exception to every rule. Sometimes you may have to cross a dangerous area if staying in your immediate surroundings will be worse for you or compromise your survival.

*You are already in a survival situation, so why take needless chances?

Assess the individual situation and make a decision accordingly.

You are what you eat

Use that space in your yard or a pot on the front porch to grow some vegetables. You will get to spend more time outside and be able to savor the amazing taste of food straight from the land, picked and delivered right to your kitchen and bursting with all the flavor and nutrients it should have.

Not only is growing and eating your own food good for you, but it also means you don't have to depend on shops and other people to feed you in times of emergency.

Many of us have experienced power failures that last for a few days and spoil everything in our refrigerators. Being able to access fresh food for extended periods of time not only will help your health but also will boost your morale.

Getting started on growing your own food

Space

There is a bit of a myth that you need a farm or a large backyard to grow your own veggies. The reality is that you don't need much space at all. A rooftop, a deck, a small flower bed, or even a few pots on your balcony are enough to grow something to add to your next meal.

Sun

Ideally, find a spot that gets sun all year round. It's okay if it gets shade for part of the year, but the more sun, the better.

Soil

There are some new methods of growing plants that don't involve soil, but we are going to keep it simple and easy for your first foray into growing your own food. You either will already have a patch of ground with soil or will need to bring in soil.

If you have a patch of ground, the first thing you will need to do is clear it to get it ready for your new plants. This involves removing any weeds or plants that are already growing there. Any large plants can be transplanted to a pot or patch of soil out of your veggie patch's way. Also remove any rocks that are larger than a fingernail, as veggies don't do well in rocky soil.

The thing with soil is that it can be very low in nutrients. So low, in fact, that your plants won't grow. This is probably the case with most inner-city soil patches. In these cases, you will need to add nutrients to the soil. This can be done in a variety of ways. I am not a fan of adding any manufactured chemicals to my soil. My preferred methods of enriching the soil include the following:

- I bring in dark, rich soil from elsewhere and mix it with my garden soil.
- I have a compost bin where I have deposited all my organic food scraps from the kitchen. These

scraps gradually break down into compost that can be mixed into the soil.

- Animal manure. Quite often you will be able to find farms that sell bags of animal manure for a pretty reasonable price. It is an excellent addition to your soil, and the smell fades over a week or so, leaving your veggies with some amazing nutrition to help them grow.
- Worms enrich soil by aerating it, allowing moisture to penetrate deeper into the ground. Their droppings also add nutrients to the soil. If you don't have any worms in your soil, it is a good indication that the soil is suffering.

As well as nutrients, the soil needs to be aerated, so make sure that you break up the first three inches of topsoil with a fork or trowel so that it is soft and workable before you plant anything in it.

Water

Much like our own bodies, plants need a good amount of water to grow. The soil should be damp to the touch but not soggy. Plants can also die of overwatering, as their roots will get moldy and break down, so use your fingertips to test how damp the soil is and adjust your watering accordingly.

Another good thing to think about is what the weather is doing. If it is hot, the plants will need more water. If it is cold and rainy, they will need less.

What to grow?

Different vegetables grow better at different times of year. The best way to figure out when to plant is to ask your local nursery or hop on the Internet and search for information about it.

Seeds versus seedlings

I remember shopping with my mom for seeds to plant in my window box so that I would have an amazing flowering garden in the spring. I always thought that planting a vegetable garden involved poking a hole in the ground, putting the seed in it, and covering it up all "Johnny Appleseed" style. Now I know that you can buy seedlings that someone else has gone to the trouble of planting and nurturing first. So how do you decide whether to buy the seeds or the baby plants?

Some vegetables don't transplant well, which means that if you bought them already established and tried to plant them in your garden, they would die. These are mainly the root crops, such as carrots, potatoes, beets, parsnips, and onions.

Apart from these types of crops, wherever possible, buy the seedlings. It is easier to plant them directly into the garden and also allows for a shorter growing season, meaning you will be eating your own homegrown vegetables even sooner.

Gardening in pots

Growing veggies in pots is a little more limiting than gardening in an outside plot, as some vegetables need more space to grow both outward and downward than a pot can provide. Carrots, for example, will be short, stunted, and stubby if you try to grow them in pots. Vegetables that work well in pots include peppers, tomatoes, beans, lettuce, squash, onions, radishes, and most edible herbs.

Pots need to have a drainage system (holes in the bottoms of the pots), and the soil should be set up in a certain way to encourage optimum growth. First, layer the bottom of the pot with about an inch of gravel. Then use a medium-weight potting soil to fill the rest of the pot.

You can purchase potting soil from a nursery or garden store as opposed to just using the soil from your yard outside. It will contain all the right nutrients to help your vegetables grow without any of the weeds or contaminants that may be present in the soil from your yard.

Decide whether you want to plant seeds or seedlings and then plant away. These pots will need to be watered once a day, but remember to test the soil with your fingers to make sure that it is damp but not soggy.

There is nothing like eating the first mouthful of your own homegrown vegetables. These basics will get you started and produce results. You will wonder why you waited so long to try it.

Cook your own

One cool thing that I think would really help in a long-term survival situation is knowing how to grow your own foods and being able to prepare food from scratch.

Now, if you are like me, you will probably say that it is just common sense, knowing how to make food from scratch. Anyone can do it. It's more a case of choosing not to, as it takes a bit longer. Well, having recently spent some time with teenagers, I'm going to say (although it makes me feel a little old) that my idea of common-sense cooking no longer applies. Kids these days (did I say I sound old?) don't really know how to boil an egg or whip up a basic pasta sauce from tomatoes and onions. It's skills like these that are going to come in handy if the electricity is down for a good length of time and supermarket foods have been depleted or have gone rotten.

Microwave meals and takeout food usually aren't the healthiest options. You don't know who prepared your meal or the condition of the food or of the kitchen where it was prepared. Takeout and processed food also usually have a whole load of additives that keep them fresher until your consumption. Your food at home doesn't have any of that. You can control every ingredient and the quality and freshness of it all. Cooking your own food saves you money and also leads to a greater appreciation of what you are consuming.

Knowing how to cook is an extremely handy skill to have even if your life doesn't depend on it. It allows you to control your own health and nutrition.

And for those who are counting calories, cooking at home allows you to have control over portion sizes and keeps you away from a whole menu of tantalizing but fatty treats.

So cook a meal from scratch at least once a week from ingredients you have grown or bought fresh from the supermarket. It's actually pretty easy, very rewarding, and usually much better for you.

Making a meal in the city

It may surprise you to learn that there are lots of edible plants growing in the city. Here are a few examples:

MUSTARD PLANTS

A common yellow flowering plant that you often see all over the side of the road has edible flowers that have quite a spicy kick. The new leaves are also good for salads and very high in vitamins A, C, and K.

SUNFLOWERS

The raw seeds are very high in protein, and the flower buds (before they bloom) can be cooked and eaten like artichokes.

DANDELIONS

The young leaves can be used for salads. They are high in calcium, magnesium, and iron. The roots, when dried and ground, make a good substitute for coffee.

THISTLES

The stalks can be eaten if you peel and boil them. The roots can be dug up and eaten raw or cooked.

STINGING NETTLE

Make sure you don't get stung collecting the leaves. But once they are boiled, the irritant is gone and they taste like spinach. Nettle leaves have all the nutrition of that dark green veggie as well.

Remember, there are far more edible plants in the world than there are poisonous ones, but you need to make only one mistake and it can be fatal. So do make sure you know what you are eating before you chow down.

Making a meal by the sea

If I ever had a choice about where to be stranded, I would choose the seaside. Apart from the possible problem of finding fresh water, the ocean provides an abundance of culinary possibilities.

There are no poisonous seaweeds. Out of the thousands of seaweed varieties in the world, none have proved to be deadly to humans. Now, I'm not saying they all taste nice and go down easily, but they will not kill you. The edible seaweeds that we find in supermarkets have usually been boiled, tenderized, and then dried to leave them in an edible state. But if you are dying of starvation, you may find that you are less fussy and more inclined to chew your way through some tough weeds that you find on the beach. And they just may sustain you until help arrives.

Some varieties of seaweed can act as laxatives, so it is best to consume this marine vegetable only in small amounts until you figure out the effect it has on your body.

The other exciting thing about ocean environments is that there is usually a wide variety of shellfish available on the tidal rocks by the shoreline.
These are often in the form of mollusks, such as
mussels and clams clinging to the rocks, and are

generally submerged at high tide and exposed at low tide.

These shellfish can be cracked open and eaten raw and provide a good source of protein. They can also be placed in their shell on a fire. When the shell opens up, they are ready to eat. It is better to cook them if you can, but in the event that you haven't been able to get a fire going, raw is okay.

Cockles also make a good meal and can be found by standing where the waves are hitting the beach and twisting your feet into the wet sand. As you sink, you should be able to find the cockles with your toes and dig them up. Sometimes you will accidentally unearth a crab hiding in the sand. You will know this because it will give your toe a good, sharp nip. Don't be scared; just dig down and grab the crab. They are better eating than the cockles!

Now, the obvious option that I have left out here is fish! Fish are very tasty, but unless you have come prepared with a fishing line and hooks or a spear and some goggles, your chances of catching them are slim. It is a very hard task to catch a fish in the ocean without the proper tools, and your time and energy would be best spent gathering food in rock pools and along the shoreline.

Warning

The ocean has been more polluted by humans than the rest of the planet. It works furiously to clean out what we are dumping into it daily. Much like the trees are the lungs of the earth, seaweed helps filter the toxic waste out of the ocean in an effort to cleanse it. Shellfish also filter such waste. Please don't try to eat the raw produce of the sea near heavily populated areas, as it can make you sick. This edible advice is only for severe survival situations where your choice of food is limited and you are well away from civilization.

Making a meal in the desert

The desert would have to be one of my least favorite places to be stranded (apart from a glacier), but since you don't usually get a say where you end up in an unexpected situation, I am definitely going to cover it.

Most people picture deserts as devoid of life (cut to sounds of wind and pictures of tumbleweeds). The truth is that deserts can be teeming with life—life that you can eat. As long as you avoid spiders, crazy-colored insects, and the fanged end of most snakes, you can go to town on anything you find. I'm not saying that desert food is for the faint-hearted, as it consists mainly of insects and reptiles, but you will get enough to survive.

INSECTS

Ants are edible, as are termites, locusts, and grasshoppers. A bushy branch will provide a great swatter to stun the locust to the ground long enough for you to grab it. Pull the head off and the guts will come with it. Eat what remains. It's better cooked, but raw will do. Dead tree trunks will provide you with grubs or larvae that you can chow down raw too, but they taste a bit nicer cooked.

FLORA

For your vegetables, you may be lucky enough to come across a cactus or two. The fruit of most cacti are sweet and edible, but they come with a strong deterrent. Just ask Baloo from *The Jungle Book*. Unless you have a way of scraping the prickles off the fruit, I would avoid eating them. You don't want these prickles in your skin or down your throat. And it's not the big, obvious ones that are the issue. There are small, fine spikes that are harder to see and that can cause the most grief.

You can eat the leaves or pads of most cacti, but you will need to de-spike and peel the outer layer away. Eat them in moderation, as they may have a laxative effect.

REPTILES

Lizards are a good food source, but you need to be able to cook them before eating, as they can carry

all sorts of bacteria and parasites that are not good for human consumption.

Snakes are edible, but it's not worth the risk of catching them first. It takes only one wrong move and the snake wins.

Most of the larger desert animals, such as coyotes, foxes, and rabbits, come out at night. They tend to move fast and have the advantage of night vision. Usually, the calories spent chasing them down are not worth the payoff in the end.

Remember, you could live for a week off the residents of a termite mound, so ignore the idea of what you are eating and tuck in. Your rescue team will be glad you did.

Making a meal out of plants

If the idea of killing your own food and perhaps eating it raw is more than you can bear, then never fear. There are a lot of edible plants to choose from. The other bonus is that plants are far easier to collect, as they won't try to run away.

Most plants are edible, but the poisonous ones can do severe damage and even kill you. Do a course with an expert to learn how to identify the edible ones. Make sure you know what you are eating before you chow down.

If you don't know what you are doing, a good rule of thumb is, don't eat any plants with the following features:

- mushrooms or fungi (not even if you think they are magical)
- milky or discolored sap
- beans, bulbs, or seeds inside pods
- bitter or soapy taste (won't really be appealing, anyway)
- spines, fine hairs, or thorns (not good for the tongue)
- an almond scent (think marzipan)
- grains with pink, purple, or black spikes on them

- three-leaved growth pattern—that is, three leaves on the same twig stem (I would also avoid touching them, as they may well be poison oak or poison ivy.)

Protein

Animals are a great source of protein and energy. Unfortunately, they usually require a large amount of energy and planning to catch. They will sustain you for a good amount of time, though, so by all means, trap, spear, outrun, or bludgeon anything

that you can in order to survive (humans are not included in that equation).

Remember to cut out the digestive tract immediately after killing, as it can poison the meat. And then cook thoroughly. It is better to have very well-done meat in the wild, as wild animal flesh can harbor bacteria and parasites that meat from your supermarket does not.

Starving by mid-morning?

Research shows that you can survive for about three days without water and about three weeks without food. But let me tell you from experience, after ten days of no food you are pretty much as useful as a moldy carrot. So I'm going to say you have about ten good survival days in you with no food and two good days with no water.

For those of you who have ever hiked in the northern part of South Australia, you know that although it is a barren, dry place, there are a few hidden water holes that remain full (usually), even in the driest of seasons. Since every liter of water weighs one kilogram (2.2 pounds), carting all your water in for an extended trip would require you to carry a pack that would simply get too heavy to lift. I would always carry a minimum of six liters on trips into these areas, but there is often a need to rely on water holes.

A friend and I had headed into this region for a four-day excursion to practice my navigation techniques, as I had my hiking instructor's exam coming up. At the end of day two, we planned to refill at a water hole that we knew of. Although it had been a particularly dry summer, I had seen this water hole full in worse times. As you can guess, we got to the water hole and it was totally dry and dusty, with not a drop to be found. But that was okay because, like all good hiking guides, we had a backup plan: there was a well about a kilometer away. We hastily packed up and began the hike to the well. It was getting dark by then. We made it to the well by dusk and started pumping. Nothing. The well was dry.

After checking our map we realized that our only option was to hike out to the car the next day. The other water holes that we could aim for would take us only farther into the park, and if they too were dry we would be in real trouble. We had only half a liter of water between us as it was. We ate the food we had and swallowed a few mouthfuls of warm water that really didn't even begin to slake our thirst.

The next day was going to be more than one hundred degrees Fahrenheit. We packed up early and headed out before the heat could set in, but we were already dehydrated from the day before. As the day got hotter we tried to just take a small mouthful of water here and there, but it was not enough.

The first thing that goes with heatstroke is your capacity for reasoning—you become disoriented and confused. To change my navigation skills, we had deliberately chosen a route that neither of us had done before and with no set path. I began to notice that I was staring at the map but nothing seemed to make sense. I stopped paying attention to our surroundings, as I needed all my brain capacity to put one foot in front of the other. We were soon lost. Thank goodness we realized this quite quickly and sat down in the shade to regroup. After a good deal of deliberating, we figured out where we thought we were and decided on a new route out.

Lucky for us, we were right. About two hours later, we found the car and the spare water. Our legs were like rubber. I don't know how much longer it would have been before we became dysfunctional out there. We probably had only another hour or so in us. I have hiked for a few days without food before, but I would not have gotten through another day with no water.

Fears and facts

Most of our fears are based on false beliefs or ignorance. Both outdoor guiding and stunt performing has brought me into contact with a lot of people facing their fears. From what I have seen, there are two main ways to develop fears. One way is to have experienced something that has led you to fear it. The other way is to have fears instilled in you by someone else. In some cases, people have absolutely no idea why they fear something, but this is usually quite rare.

If you have been in a plane crash, it is very understandable that you would be scared of flying. If you have been bitten by a dog, it is understandable that you may not like dogs. These are cases where you have experienced something traumatic and now it scares you.

More common is having fear instilled in you. This sounds much more traumatic than it is. I'm not talking about the "if you don't behave, the bogeyman will get you" sort of instilling. I am talking about inheriting the fears of the people around us. Usually, it comes from our parents. We generally want to be like the people we idolize when we are growing up. This includes liking what they like, not liking what they don't, and fearing what they do. How many of you are scared of something that your mother is scared of as well?

I often saw this when I was working as a rock-climbing instructor. I would sometimes work at an indoor wall and do kids' parties. This involved belaying (holding the rope) and keeping the kids safe while they clambered up the climbing wall. We would chat to the kids as a group and make sure that they felt reassured before the whole process began.

Now, kids are natural climbers. They don't fear getting on that wall (an adult class is a whole different matter). But I would see this scenario time and time again:

A child is happily climbing up the wall for the second or third time. Her mom has missed our introductory talk and wanders into the gym to see how her child is doing. She sees her daughter half-way up the wall and starts to panic. She calls up to

*How many of your fears are based on fact? It may be time to do some research.

her child and says that it's okay if she doesn't want to go to the top. The mother's fear begins to influence the child, and before long, she's in tears, saying that she wants to come down. I lower her down, and she now thinks climbing is way too scary and doesn't want to try it again.

Here's another scenario. I worked with a girl (let's call her "Emma") to help her overcome her fear of birds. When I asked Emma why she was so petrified of them, she couldn't really give me a reason. The most that she could come up with was something about them being dirty and diseased, and that her mom was scared of them.

I told her that we humans are more likely to kill birds with the diseases we carry than the other way around. Avian flu is usually transmitted through bird droppings that are spread through things like air-conditioning ducts. You're more likely to catch bird diseases in your office than from coming into contact with any birds.

Over the period of a few weeks, Emma slowly overcame her fear of birds to the point that she held one at an aviary. I brought her mother along to the aviary too, and she also was able to overcome her prejudice against our feathered friends. Emma's mother was trying to pinpoint where her fear came from and could remember her mother telling her that birds were diseased. And so the myth had been passed down from generation to generation.

Emma recently tweeted me a photo of a bird with the caption, "Isn't he cute?" I'm guessing she doesn't hate them so much now.

Regular check on expiration dates

Remember that things like canned goods, emergency supplies, and first aid items usually have a use-by date, so check through your stocks every few months and replace anything that is no longer good. If you use something from your emergency stash (such as candles in a blackout), restock it as soon as the emergency has passed.

Domestic fires

SOMETIMES FIRE PLUS WATER = EVEN BIGGER FIRE

We have all been taught that water puts out fire. This means that when we see something on fire in the home, our first instinct is to rush to the tap and douse the flames with water. In fact, this can lead to disastrous consequences if the cause of the fire is something electrical or oil. In each of these cases water will actually intensify the fire rather than put it out.

The bottom line? Stop and look. A quick glance should allow you enough time to figure out the cause of the flames. Anything on fire on the stove will probably be oil or grease. Anything sparking will probably be electrical. If you are unsure, don't use water.

Unless the fire is very small and easily contained, always call the fire department. Fires can quickly get out of control, so the sooner the fire department is there, the better. No one will tell you off if you manage to get it under control before they get there, and it's much better to be safe than sorry.

OIL FIRES

An oil fire on the stove tends to burn out quite quickly. If it doesn't, grab the baking soda out of your pantry and douse the flames with that. (Make sure you don't grab the flour by mistake, as that will make the fire worse.) The very worst you will end up with is a pan that needs washing, rather than the loss of all that you own.

If you are running out of baking soda, a damp towel will also smother grease flames, but it needs

to be damp (not dripping). If it is too dry it may just add fuel to your fire.

ELECTRICAL FIRES

The first thing you will need to do (after dialing 9-1-1) is locate the main breaker box in the house. Knowing where this is located is great for a variety of other unexpected emergencies (e.g., a blown electrical fuse causing the house lights to go out), so maybe put this book down for a minute and wander around the house now to find it. It could be

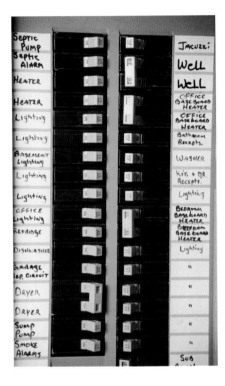

inside or outside your house. Mine is at the top of my stairs on the second floor. It is usually a gray metal box, lies flat against the wall, and looks something like this picture inside.

As well as fuses, it has a main on/off switch. This is what you will look for. Making sure that you have dry hands, flick the switch to off. If you're doing this at night, you will lose all the lights in your house too, so make sure you have a flashlight on hand.

Don't use a normal fire extinguisher to put out these kinds of fires. If you have a specific extinguisher for electrical fires (Class C or multi-purpose ABC extinguisher), use that. Most people do not have a household fire extinguisher, so the best thing to do is grab the baking soda or salt out of the cupboard and try to smother the fire with that. If the fire is spreading, chances are you will not have enough baking soda to put it out. In this case, get your family and pets out of the house and leave the fire department to do its job.

Note

Candles are one of the most common causes of house fires, so remember to place that romantic mood lighting somewhere it won't ignite the nearest houseplant, and take a second to blow out your candles before falling contentedly to sleep.

Fire first aid

I know that it seems simple, but you will be surprised by how many people forget this in the "heat" of the moment. If you have just burned yourself, then cool the burn area down.

An obvious choice for cooling down is ice. Never apply the ice directly to the skin, as ice can also burn, which just ends up making the situation worse. Wrap the ice in a tea towel or some other material, wet the material, and apply it to the burn until the heat goes out of it.

If you have no ice, cool water works well, and if you can add wind to the equation, it will work even better. Think of a stream to wet the burn and then a mountain breeze to cool it down even further, and you get the picture.

Sunstroke and sunburn are also injuries caused by heat. Use the same method. Remove the heat source (get out of the sun and move into the shade), and then cool the affected areas down (apply a cool cloth to your forehead and sip some water).

It is important to cool the area down as soon as possible, because after initial contact with the heat source, the burn may continue to affect deeper layers of skin even after the heat source has been removed.

How to pee in the woods

Shake your booty. Please don't find this gross, but it is okay for women in the outdoors to apply the shake method after peeing. It adds a little extra exercise to your day and means that you don't have to figure out what to do with your soiled tissue or toilet paper. It helps preserve toilet paper until you *really* need to use it as well.

It also means that you won't have to panic if you get stuck in a public toilet with no paper in the stall and no one to pass you some from under the door. Just wiggle it out.

Urine is actually very sanitary. It contains ammonia, which is a common disinfectant used in a lot of household cleaners. Many African tribes actually urinate on their wounds in order to sterilize them to prevent infection. Wilderness first aid courses still teach such practices today if the need is dire enough. However, if you feel like washing your hands after peeing, then carrying around a small hand sanitizer will do the trick.

How to poop in the woods

Whereas pee is sanitary, poop is anything but. Poop is a waste product that contains bacteria and disease. It needs to be disposed of properly.

There are the really hard core outdoor enthusiasts who believe we shouldn't leave anything behind in nature that wasn't there when we went in. And that's great. I'm not one of them. I believe that poop is nature's fertilizer (we use manure to grow mushrooms and roses), and it's actually contributing to nature when I leave some of it out there. In order to avoid spreading disease and ruining other people's outdoor experiences, however, it does need to be buried at least eight inches. Any shallower and it is easily dug up or exposed by the elements. For this little activity you will need a trowel or garden spade. Putting a rock pile on top of your covered hole will also keep it from being exposed.

After pooping, wash your hands! This is not optional. Poor hygiene can spread disease through your friends and family as quickly as a dirty hypodermic needle. If you have run out of any kind of soap, then a good scrubbing with sand or dirt and some water works almost as well.

Many women in stressful situations become unable to poop. This is largely due to the fact that the brain and the digestive system are strongly connected and regulated by many of the same hormones and by the nervous system. There are many women who can't even do number two in a public restroom.

Not pooping is detrimental to your health. There are more and more studies to prove that the digestive system actually helps regulate the overall health of your body. Constipation leads to toxic buildup in your body and eventually will make you sick. If you don't poop for a long enough time (and this is where it gets a little gross), a hard plug will form in your colon, and you will soon be unable to poop at all. Then the only way to get better is to insert your finger up your bottom (or have some-one else do it!) and break it up, which is way more embarrassing than pooping outdoors or in a public restroom. So please make sure you continue to try to poop at least once a day wherever you are.

Using toilet paper in the outdoors

I recommend wiping after a bout of the number twos. The toilet paper you use either will need to be carried out or burned. Coming from Australia, I am a little wary of lighting paper in the outdoors in case I set the whole bush on fire, so I prefer the paper-in-the-plastic-bag method. Some people use rocks to wipe with; just don't use sharp ones. And there is always the advocate of the leaf, but I would be really careful which ones you choose, especially in the US, where poison oak is rampant. Anything that may have poison or fine prickles should be kept well away from the wiping region. I have found that a good handful of sagebrush works best.

What to do with the toilet paper if you do use it? You would (I hope) take your garbage out of the wilderness, so why leave your toilet paper? I carry a small plastic bag that I put the toilet paper in to store until I find a trash can to dispose of it. Now, you may find this unappealing, but how many of you carry dog feces in plastic bags? If you have dug a good-sized hole for your toilet business, then it is okay to place the toilet paper in the bottom of the hole and bury it with everything else. Please don't leave it lying on top of the hole, as invariably it will blow away and litter the countryside with toilet paper "streamers." This might be okay for Halloween pranks, but it's not okay for a hike out in the great outdoors.

Periods

I have only one suggestion for used tampons: take them back out of the wilderness with you. Even if you dig a deep hole to bury them in, the smell of blood will draw the attention of some little carnivore, and soon the countryside will be littered with regurgitated tampons.

For an extended trip into the outdoors, store them in a couple of airtight plastic bags. You really don't want to be attracting any unnecessary carnivores to your camp.

It's time to dispel the popular myth that women should stay out of the outdoors when menstruating. Many studies have been done to discover whether bears are more attracted to women who are menstruating than women who are not. These studies have concluded that women on their periods do not attract more attention from bears than other people. So don't avoid the outdoors at this time of the month, and don't get fearful if you happen to be stranded out there when you are menstruating. Just pay a little bit more attention to your hygiene and dispose of the used items wisely.

Okay, so what if you get caught by surprise by your period and don't have access to tampons or pads? There are some reusable period options on the market today that might be good to throw into your first aid kit. They include sponges and the menstrual cup. Make sure if you choose to use these that you keep them sanitized. Anything that you put into your body should be very clean prior to insertion.

The fallback is, of course, what our grandmothers used to use: a piece of absorbent cloth rolled up and placed between our legs. You will need to experiment with the best material and the best thickness and comfort for your body. You will need to wash these out and have a few spares on hand for when you are waiting for the used ones to dry.

This will require planning and a little bit of extra work, but will be the best, most effective long-term solution.

Sanitation

Pooping and peeing need to be done a good distance away from water sources. I recommend a minimum of sixty feet. As mentioned before, poop carries disease, and you don't want that disease to be washed into your (or anyone else's) drinking and washing water.

There are many good suggestions for how to manage waste in a long-term survival situation, but that would be a book on its own.

Just keep in mind the old adage, "Don't poop where you eat." Make sure that you keep sanitation in mind, and establish a space that is going to be used only as a toilet area. Also be certain that the waste is well buried and disposed of away from water sources.

This includes urban environments too. Most water supplies in houses are replenished by electricity. This means that you won't be able to flush your toilets during power failures. As soon as you realize that you are in for an extended period of no power, stop using the toilets for number two and find another method of disposal. This could be using a bucket and then disposing of the contents outside, or even digging a hole in your backyard if you have one. Just think, *fertilizer* . . .

Remember

Embrace all the things that come with being a woman. You have softness and grace, but also realize that you have within you an incredible strength that will enable you to handle whatever life throws your way. Being proactive in a situation will always trump being reactive, and the more that you educate yourself about your fears, the less fearsome they will seem. Look at these methods of survival more as tools that will enable you to thrive in your everyday life rather than as things that you will use only in an emergency. Above all else, believe in yourself. You can do it.

Acknowledgments

I'd like to thank the following people:

My mum and dad, Loy and Peter Burford, for always encouraging me to pursue my dreams no matter how extreme or far-fetched they were. I always felt secure to aim high, knowing they would provide the safety net if I fell.

My amazing aunt, Jan Adams, for reading everything I wrote and reminding me of my true purpose. This book would not be what it is without her help.

Neil Jackson for always believing that I can do anything I set my mind to and then helping me do it all.

Paul Duddridge for pointing me in the right direction time and time again. I wouldn't have put pen to paper without him.

My awesome literary agent, Adriann Ranta, for taking a chance with me. She saw exactly who I was and knew what best to do with me—no small task.